EFL COMMUNICATION STRATEGIES
IN A VIRTUAL WORLD

Further titles in this series

Teaching EFL Online

The Fractal Approach to TEFL

Controversies in ELT

Developing Learner Autonomy Through Tasks

Artificial Intelligence in Autonomous Language Learning

www.linguabooks.com

EFL COMMUNICATION STRATEGIES IN A VIRTUAL WORLD

AN EXPLORATORY STUDY

Susan Gowans

Print edition: ISBN 978-1-911369-50-9
eBook edition: ISBN 978-1-911369-51-6

Second edition

This book first appeared under the title
'EFL Communication Strategies in Second Life'

Series editor: Maurice Claypole

A CIP catalogue record for this book is available from the British Library.

LinguaBooks
Elsie Whiteley Innovation Centre
Hopwood Lane
Halifax HX1 5ER
United Kingdom

www.linguabooks.com

A different species a different set of values a world completely unlike your own. There is a feeling you can only get when you meet the unknown and open your mind. – Nakajima (Gin no Saji)

– Hiromu Arakawa

About the author

Susan Gowans is a graduate of Dundee University and was awarded an MSc TESOL with distinction by the University of Edinburgh. Her career as an educator and teacher trainer has included teaching English in primary, secondary and private schools in Japan, South Korea and her native Scotland.

At the time of writing, Susan was engaged at an elementary school in South Korea, teaching conversational English from grade four to six both in the classroom and in online environments. She is passionate about all aspects of language-teaching methodology, in particular issues relating to online language learning and teaching, and has shared her insights by holding methodology workshops for serving teachers.

In addition to education, her active interests include health and nutrition, world cuisine, photography, jewellery and accessory design, as well as children's and young adult literature, in particular picture books and their potential as a powerful tool for language learning.

Abstract

This paper reports the findings of an exploratory case study examining communication strategy use between three adult EFL learners from diverse cultural backgrounds and their teacher whilst incorporating voice and text chat during meaning-focused conversation tasks in *Second Life.* The analysis of the session transcript revealed that participants employed many of the communication strategies concomitant with face-to-face interactions for effective conversation management. The data also revealed that the participants adapted their communication strategies to suit the Second Life platform, thus overcoming conversational ambiguities arising from the absence of paralinguistic signals. In addition, discourse analysis of the transcript offered further insight into power relations, politeness and risk taking and provided signs of sociocultural learning and language development in line with second language acquisition (SLA) theory. Finally, the paper concludes that the modalities provided by the Second Life platform offer learners an alternative for communication and showing presence during discussion. It also concludes that teacher facilitation and continued support is important to engage learners in the virtual environment, to mediate the acclimatisation of the new surroundings and encourage them to take risks, thus taking control of their learning and autonomous practice. It evaluates the potential of using Second Life for language teaching and learning and provides a direction for future research.

CONTENTS

Foreword to the second edition

In terms of the research presented and the author's pedagogical observations and insights, this book is as relevant today as when it was written. Whereas the Second Life metaverse is no longer widely used as a platform for language teaching, virtual worlds themselves are very much part of today's technological landscape. On the other hand, headset-based virtual reality experiences incorporating haptic technologies are still very much in their infancy. In a sense, we are still standing on the threshold of the next big breakthrough in technology-enhanced communicative language teaching.

Furthermore, recent events, in particular coronavirus lockdowns and travel restrictions, have created a new demand for socially-distanced learning solutions, and this second edition of Susan Gowans' work serves as a timely reminder that there is a world beyond Zoom and other camera-based meeting platforms – a less static, more dynamic virtual world where the opportunities for innovative and creative learning strategies are limited only by the imagination.

MC, January 2022

Foreword to the first edition

The horizons of online learning have widened considerably over the last five or six years. I will never forget the day in the spring of 2006 when during the course of creating an ad-hoc online lesson for one of my blended learning business classes, I was trawling the internet for a suitable recording of the Dolly Parton hit, "Nine to Five" and came across an amateur video showing an animated character dancing from the living room of a tastefully furnished detached house, through the kitchen and out into a picket-fenced garden, the dancer moving gracefully in time to the music. How on earth, I wondered, had this sequence been created?

A little research provided the answer and thus began my own working relationship with the 3D world of Second Life. At the time, this multiplayer online adventure scenario was in its infancy and largely unheard of outside the gaming community, but I was instantly seized by the potential for language learning and quickly set up a modest language school in Second Life to complement the regular teaching activities of my bricks and mortar school and did my best to spread the word to colleagues through a series of talks, workshops and publications.

Perhaps it was a sign of the times that more often than not, I encountered considerable scepticism from fellow teachers on both sides of the digital divide, but in fairness it must be said that at the time Second Life lacked many of the features that have since made it popular. The proprietary browser was far from stable and in many ways counter-intuitive, avatars were somewhat primitive, creating objects and handling textureswere cumbersome endeavours and more importantly, inworld chat was entirely text-based, for the introduction of voice chat was many months away.

In the interceding years, however, many improvements have been made and acceptance has increased to the extent that Second Life is now fully recognized as a communication platform and educational opportunity by many businesses and universities, and an ever-increasing number of language teachers and learners are seeking to tap into its potential. Countless experiments have since been conducted and there are now a number of successful virtual language schools operating within this borderless international community. From an academic point of view, there is a growing body of literature on the subject, but until now little attention has been paid to the communication strategies used by language learners and their teachers, and it is precisely this insight that forms the point of departure for the work carried out by Susan Gowans and presented in this book.

Originally written as a research paper for the University of Edinburgh, this study demonstrates a keen attention to detail that casts light on the way learners interact within the confines of an intercultural language lesson taking place in a three-dimensional virtual metaverse. This specialised case study is an exploration in which the immersive qualities of Second Life are both felt and observed and in which subtle power relationships are seen to shine through the linguistic interchanges of natural classroom banter.

Above all, this work presents a snapshot in Second Life time. Rather than paint the techniques used and strategies observed with a broad brush, Susan Gowans directs her attention toward a very specific instance, focusing mainly on a single session within the context of an online language course of which the Second Life sessions were just one component, investigating, as it were, the microcosm within the macrocosm. Perhaps it really is time, as Susan Gowans suggests, to re-shape how we think and learn in the light of the way interaction evolves through technological changes and multi-modalities.

Whether you are a teacher, researcher or interested bystander, this book provides a great deal of food for thought and reveals that beneath the routine interaction between language learners and their teacher, and indeed amongst the learners themselves, there is a wealth of hidden detail from which the careful observer can draw a number of meaningful and sometimes surprising conclusions.

Maurice Claypole BA MA (Lond), Cert Ed, MCIL, MCollT, AITI, PhD
September 2012

Acknowledgements

First of all, I would like to express my gratitude to those who helped make my original dissertation possible. Without the support and encouragement from my family, friends and certain members of staff in the MSc TESOL program, it would not have been possible to complete the work.

In particular, I am sincerely grateful to my supervisor, Ruby Rennie, for her expertise, warm nature and the continued support she provided throughout the writing process. Indeed, I am extremely fortunate to have such a supervisor who helped build my confidence and gave me the freedom to explore on my own whilst providing the necessary guidance to meet my goals. Most of all, I am truly indebted and thankful to my partner and colleague, Andy Webster, for believing in me and urging me to never give up. If it was not for his inspiring passion for his online EFL course, *Global Imaginarium,* I would never have been able to collect such insightful data. Likewise, I would like to express my heartfelt gratitude to my immediate and extended family, who have been a constant source of love and strength throughout this endeavour.

Finally, my thanks go to Ann Claypole at LinguaBooks for preparing and revising the manuscript and to Maurice Claypole for editorial suggestions and making publication possible.

Chapter 1: Introduction

1.1. *General introduction*

This research study sets out to demonstrate that Second Life (SL) is a legitimate pedagogical tool for effective language development and that it can be used to engage learners from diverse cultural backgrounds in the negotiation of meaning and thereby provide adult EFL learners and educators with new opportunities to practice or facilitate English.

This chapter delivers an overview of what SL is and why using SL is a viable pedagogical tool for educators. It also identifies the rationale and purpose of the study.

1.2. *Overview of Second Life*

Wankel and Kingsley (2009) explain that there are more than one hundred active virtual worlds and Second Life (also referred to as a MUVE – a Multi-User Virtual Environment) is the most popular (Warburton, 2009). In particular, it has been recognised among educators for its educational potential; however, its 'instructional strategies' remain in question (Keskitalo et al., 2011; Warburton, 2009; Salmon, 2009). SL is often compared to Massively Multiplayer Online Role Playing Games (MMORPGs) such as *World of Warcraft*. However, while it shares common features in that it "supports role-playing game communities" (Warburton, 2009: 416), SL is not a game because there are no "predetermined narrative or plot-driven storylines" (ibid.). SL is best described as a synchronous 3D social networking environment where people all over the world can communicate through their avatars – virtual figures which represent their users. Nevertheless, SL is limited to those with a fast internet connection and enough computer capacity to able to handle the demands of the software. If users have the equipment necessary to take part in this virtual network, they can download and use SL for free and are therefore open to a variety of creative uses from buying land, designing and building contents to transforming identities. In addition, users create content to which they retain property rights and which they can sell, exchange or donate to other SL residents.

In terms of education, it is believed that virtual worlds provide educators with new possibilities for thinking about pedagogy, which Salmon confirms:

> *SL is experiential, collaborative and immersive in ways that no virtual learning environment (VLE) or remote synchronous classroom ever could be ... it is important in the future for academics to experience SL in order to understand the potential and, especially, SL's affordances that enable exploration and discovery.* (2009: 529)

It is also suggested that the anonymity in virtual worlds can have a positive impact on the learner as Freiermuth (cited in Ranalli, 2008: 442) asserts that "with respect to affective barriers, computer simulations incorporating synchronous chat can motivate learners who would normally be shy in face-to-face interaction to contribute more actively." It has also been suggested that, "the immersive nature of the virtual world, crossing physical, social and cultural dimensions, can provide a compelling educational experience, particularly in relation to simulation and role-playing activities" (Warburton, 2009: 419). Salmon contends that because of the blurring of boundaries between fantasy and reality often experienced in SL, "individuals may engage in activities that they would not undertake in real life" (2009: 533). In addition, the use of SL gives rise to instant communication for those less inclined to communicate via asynchronous platforms such as email or discussion forums. Furthermore, the Real Life (RL) or physical distance between learners enforces a need for synchronous instant communication. Whilst there are many communicative platforms available to educators which are more user-friendly, SL has been shown to enhance motivation in most learners because of visual stimulations and the existence of avatars, which evoke a wide range of authentic conversation (Omale et al., 2009). Therefore, for second language instructors and learners alike, such an environment can provide an indispensable tool with language-learning benefits. By embracing a paradigm shift in digital education and engaging in digital literacies, it can create a new way of thinking about texts. It can open up new and innovative ways to bring technology into education and highlight the affordances of a variety of experiences in different domains (Burnett, 2009).

1.3. Rationale: background and purpose of the study

The purpose of this study is to contribute to the literature on language learning in virtual worlds by considering the potential of learning and practising English in SL. It will provide a holistic and constructivist account of how appropriately designed conversational tasks can engage learners in meaningful negotiation whilst offering a pedagogical tool to assist in language learning. The present study encapsulates social constructivist and interactionist principles, which Girvan and Savage (2010) assert is “an obvious pedagogy for use in virtual worlds which have tools that afford the building of objects in a flexible and persistent environment”. Many efforts have been made to engage culturally diverse EFL learners across time zones who find difficulty communicating in English with native or non-native speakers on a daily basis. Within this controlled online learning environment, the aim is to encourage sociocultural patterns to emerge, which Lantolf (2000) suggests is an important consideration as a way of heightening language development.

Whilst efforts have been made to explore, evaluate and test the affordances of foreign language learning in virtual worlds, one area that appears under-explored in this context is the use of communication strategies among adult EFL learners and their teacher and how they adapt to the features of virtual platforms for effective communication, interactional development, exchange of meaning and interpersonal communication. This dissertation presents an exploratory case study utilizing SL to examine the interactional strategies unique to this context and environment where paralinguistic, non-verbal cues are absent. Therefore, the research questions which aim to shape the current study are as follows:

1. Out of the selected communication strategies, which do the participants employ most during meaning-focused interaction in Second Life?

2. What significant themes emerge from analysis of communication strategy use during the Second Life session?

3. How is Second Life used for efficient conversational management during group discussion when para-linguistic communication strategies are limited?

By examining the communication strategy use amongst the participants – both learners and their teacher – the current study also highlights how such an environment can help language facilitation and learning and how it acts as an aid to risk taking by examining the relationship between this context and communication strategy use in accordance with second language acquisition (SLA) theory.

Chapter 2: Literature review

2.1. *Introduction*

This chapter reviews research on the use of computer-mediated communication (CMC) and virtual worlds within educational contexts, thus presenting how past research has informed the present study. The themes discussed are: *language learning in computer-mediated contexts, educational research in virtual environments, language learning in Second Life and its potential drawbacks* and finally, the *rationale for the use of communication strategies in CMC contexts.* On the basis of this review, Chapter 3 will then go on to discuss the methodology appropriate for the present study.

2.2. *Language learning in computer-mediated communication contexts*

The growing interest in researching MUVEs in language education is believed to have evolved from the vast range of studies in both computer-assisted language learning (CALL) and computed-mediated communication (CMC). Social platforms such as Facebook, multimodal digital literacy platforms, online chat, email, blogs and wikis have provided language learners with increased opportunities to engage in authentic communication with native speakers in the target language. The increased use of such platforms is progressively being recognised by practitioners as a powerful means for classroom use thereby acknowledging "the power of informal learning and its like to powerful practises with digital text" (Robinson and Carrington, 2009: 6).

It is believed that synchronous CMC environments can provide second language learners with encouraging benefits and an improved understanding of their potential as an aid to learning (Warschauer, 1996). In particular, the immersive nature of CMC contexts can encourage interaction amongst learners whereby it is "necessary to view the second language learner as essentially a social being, taking part in structured social networks and social practices" (Mitchell and Myles, 2004: 27). This view, in turn, is seen as an essential ingredient for successful language learning.

Thus, the further advantages of CMC contexts have been observed to enhance "out-put, motivation and risk taking" (Peterson, 2010: 274). Warschauer (1997) documented that text-based CMC provides learners with a medium to encourage closer attention to linguistic form, essential for effective foreign language acquisition (Schmidt, 1990). It has also been shown to provide a less stressful learning environment, consequently reducing anxiety associated with language learning because learners demonstrate fewer signs of socially debilitating factors such as "age, gender, social hierarchy and isolation" (Hundsberger, 2009: 4), which are factors commonly found in real-life traditional classroom settings worldwide. Learners and educators/facilitators have demonstrated that they have more freedom to express themselves within CMC environments and are less afraid of being judged by others (Overbaugh and Lin 2006). Salmon further claims that "tutors' avatars interacting with students' avatars within the immersive SL environment created an equal relationship, breaking down the old tutor-student hierarchical relationships [...] The development of equal relationships, where preconceptions about who is who change, contribute to the start of a virtual third culture" (2011: 75).

Further emphasised is the data recording effectiveness of computer mediated teaching. Conversation transcripts provide educators with a convenient means for efficient error correction and also practitioner reflections (Lee, 2001). In addition, studies have shown how appropriate CMC environments are for task-based learning because of their learner-centred nature (Jauregi et al., 2011). This has, consequently, demonstrated innovative task design potential for educators in a variety of fields.

Despite the many learning potentials CMC environments encourage, it is understood that by merely introducing a new CM tool into a teaching programme, it is not expected to "radiate learning" (de Freitas et al., 2010). It is important to consider how the technology can help "integrate a community and how communities influence the use of technologies" (Wenger et al., 2009: 13). With this view, Wenger et al. affirms that "[c]ommunitites of practice offer a useful perspective on technology because they are not defined by personal characteristics, but by people's potential to learn together" (2009: 11).

To appreciate the affordances of such environments and to uncover the language learning potentials, various authors highlight that further investigation is essential to evaluate the variables in CMC platforms (Baralt and Gruzynski-Weis, 2011; Conrad, 2002; Hurd, 2007; Peterson, 2010; Keskitalo et al., 2011). These include the relatively unexplored "individual, interactive, goal-oriented, collaborative, conversational, and immersive characteristics" (Keskitalo et al., 2011: 19).

2.3. *Educational research in virtual environments*

Research in virtual worlds such as SL provides educators, within a range of subjects, an indication of its educational possibilities (Deutschmann et al., 2009; Keskitalo, 2011; Petrakou, 2010; Schiller, 2009; Sherblom et al., 2009; Warburton, 2009). For example, it has been noted that in SL, learners can explore and experience different cultures by visiting locations, which would otherwise prove difficult in their real lives. This, in turn, offers a functional and immersive environment for authentic and experiential learning (Salmon, 2011). Research has provided insight into learners' perceptions of learning in SL stating that preference lies in collaborative activities, which exploit the virtual context's aspects of immersion (Brown, 2008; Jarmon and Sanchez, 2008; Wang et al., 2009). What is more, virtual worlds are viewed as effective tools in mediating informal and professional relationships, for managing efficient group collaboration and for brainstorming (Sherblom, 2009). Brown states that the immersive qualities remain at the heart of all learning experiences and proposes, "virtual worlds may now enable us to learn by immersion in many fields, along with other learners. We can learn from and with them, in virtual space." (Brown, 2008 cited in Salmon, 2009: 402).

Interesting accounts of potentially positive higher educational occurrences in virtual worlds are provided (see Wankel and Kingsley, 2009). In particular, they have been shown to motivate and engage learners within group discussions and provide an environment, whilst still in its infancy, which supports academic standards despite the extra effort required to participate (Ball and Pearce, 2009). In addition, a study by Girvan and Savage (2010), who sought to explore the affordances of social constructivism as pedagogy in virtual worlds, designed tasks to encourage participant groups to build on and learn from subsequent groups' artefacts. Consequently, significant signs of social constructivism emerged because of the nature of the task. In addition, signs of communal constructivism also emerged towards the end of the study. Participants highlighted the importance of passing on information to future groups, which in turn indicated the learners' need for scaffolding and further reflected the presence of communal constructivism in that they are not only building knowledge for themselves but also to benefit future groups. Interestingly, the participants' perceptions of collaborating in the virtual world unanimously came to the conclusion that the impact of the learning experience would be lost and feel more contrived when collaborating in alternative multi modal platforms, such as wikis and Virtual Learning Environments (VLEs). Therefore, it could be said that the participants in this study felt the immediacy of the synchronous immersive nature and benefited from shared visual space when carrying out tasks.

This learner-centred interactive learning has been heavily supported within CMC contexts and in particular in MUVEs, especially in facilitating group dynamics between learners who are geographically dispersed. They have been shown to provide a strong sense of group presence resulting from the shared visual space in which learners interact (Franceschi et al., 2009). In terms of task participation, the empirical study by Franceschi et al., (2009) revealed that there were significantly higher levels of engagement and participation in the virtual world as opposed to synchronous text-based virtual environments and showed similarities to classroom-based communication – still a significantly positive outcome and "a good proxy for classroom interactions regarding the level of engagement engendered" (ibid.: 95). They believe the reason for this result is because the learners engage in the task within the same physical boundaries in the traditional classroom setting and also share the same sources of distraction, thereby being simultaneously distracted. It can also be said that because of this physically shared environment, the learners are more sensitive to movements and non-verbal signals than those experienced in the virtual world and therefore have the potential to hinder the learning process. Despite this, it was also noted that this increased engagement within the virtual world collaborative task could have been a result of 'novelty bias' in that they were not motivated by the concept of the task but by simply completing it in the virtual world, a context where the participants had very little previous experience. They also stated that merely implementing the use of virtual worlds for task completion is not the best long-term solution for educational goals. Franceschi et al. (2009) therefore suggest that further research in the development of task characteristics best suited to virtual worlds is essential, which should result in more effective and valid outcomes.

2.4. *Language learning in SL and its potential drawbacks*

In terms of Computer Assisted Language Learning, research in MUVEs, the evidence still remains quite scarce. However, the few studies that have been conducted successfully have shown inspiring results and findings identifying the predominant benefits for language learning (Campbell, 2009; Deutschman et al., 2009; Deutschman and Panichi, 2009; Henderson et al., 2009; Molka-Danielsen et al., 2009; Periera, 2008; Peterson, 2009; Peterson, 2010; Petrakou, 2010; Wang et al., 2009; Jauregi et al.,

2011). One of the key reasons noted for integrating their use in language education is the social-constructivist nature they encourage in that virtual worlds allow for authentic language use through social interaction and collaborations because of their effective immersion and experiential nature. They allow learners who communicate across geographic boundaries within diverse time zones, an enhanced negotiation of meaning similar to that in real life situations thus creating content not limited to the teacher (Campbell, 2009).

Notwithstanding, there are also contradictory opinions and results regarding the use of SL in education,

> *As a virtual world it is currently not adequate as a learning environment on its own. There is a need to construct an additional information space in order to gather all information regarding the course and to display this information outside the rather distracting, graphically rich and socially dynamic virtual environment.* (Petrakou, 2010: 1027)

It is also important to acknowledge the negative implications of such environments in order to ensure such drawbacks are avoided or taken into consideration when implementing MUVEs in educational practice. For example, a newcomer to a virtual world can experience frustration in that, while there are communities open to the public, they are often difficult to find. Furthermore, participation in these communities can, at times, prove a challenge when residents are faced with communication constraints such as diverse time zones and in some cases, they lack the necessary computer competence to participate effectively (Warschauer, 2007; Warburton, 2009). What is more, it was noted that group meetings cannot only induce stress because of technological issues but they also require more patience, effort and attention than in more natural face-to-face discussions. Sherblom's study (2009) highlights the communication challenges his participants faced in Second Life which include difficulty in gaining access to SL, distractions whilst 'in-world' and notably challenges with computer lag, which was shown to hinder the natural flow of group communication. Additionally, while studies indicate that virtual worlds provide a virtual environment whereby participants are allowed to feel a closer sense of interpersonal communication, "presence, co-presence and place-presence" (Jarmon et al., 2009: 225) Sherblom (ibid.) reported that this interpersonal communication was made more difficult partly because of the lack of non-verbal cues, which also drew concern to issues surrounding anonymity and deception. However, this sensitivity, while negative, can be argued to concur with a sense of social presence which Jarmon argues to be a somewhat predominantly positive feature which virtual worlds embody (ibid.).

Whilst technological hindrances can detract from learners obtaining the full potential of this rich language learning environment (Berge, 2008; de Freitas et al., 2010; Keskitalo et al., 2011; Petrakou, 2010; Sherblom et al., 2009), it has been suggested that in order to utilise the virtual platform most effectively and thus help learners to overcome feelings of frustration when using SL, it is important to offer them sufficient support and scaffolding during orientation. Sherblom (2009) informs that such orientation should not only include assisting learners to develop competence with the technology, but should also introduce them to strategies to engage with others through the medium. They should also develop interpersonal communication skills and communicate effectively in groups, which will lessen the feelings of limited expression following the lack of non-verbal cues.

Many researchers see the lack of face-to-face contact as a debilitating factor in effective communication competence. However Walther et al., (2005) offer insight into the evidence of how learners overcome such absence of paralinguistic cues. They indicate that interlocutors display increased signs of adjusting their communication strategies when non-verbal cues are absent in synchronous communication in order to meet communication ends. In this case, they state that interlocutors use more verbal than non-verbal cues to express how they feel, therefore indicating that it is possible to feel less affected by the distance when communicating in CMC contexts and learn to successfully develop, over time, the "social-emotional and relational information" needed for building meaningful relationships. Using SL in a pedagogically appropriate way and providing the learners with initial training, opens them up to the potential of practicing effective critical thinking, interactive and collaborative learning, enhanced sociocultural awareness and understanding as well as an increased sense of presence and social inclusion (Jarmone and Sanchez, 2008; Jarmon et al., 2009; Salmon, 2009; Walther et al., 2005; Warschauer, 2003; Wenger, 1998).

2.5. *Rationale for the use of communication strategies in CMC contexts*

The study of communication strategies (CSs) has been given considerable attention and in particular in second language use

(Bialystock, 1990; Dreyer and Oxford, 1996; O'Malley and Chamot, 1990; Oxford, 2003; Tarone, 1981; Yule and Tarone, 1997). In terms of research in virtual worlds, there is little examination of the role of communication strategies between student/student and teacher/student interaction, which leads Peterson (2010) to state that further research in this area would be highly beneficial. Therefore, the present study aims not only to contribute to the literature of language learning and language use in virtual worlds, but also to add to the developing literature surrounding communication strategy use in Second Life.

CSs are inherent in foreign or second language interaction as a way to avoid communication breakdown between interlocutors. Ellis (1994) asserts that such strategies are primarily used to alleviate lexical and grammatical problems and are employed by the language learners when they cannot retrieve the resources essential to express the meaning they want to convey. They are not consciously learned linguistic items, but rather "they are descriptive of the learners' pattern of *use* of what they know as they try to communicate with speakers of the TL" (Tarone, 1981: 287 *italics in original*). O'Malley and Chamot (1990) add that CSs are also used between interlocutors who do not share the same linguistic competence, for instance, communication between the second language learner and a speaker of the target language. Importantly, Tarone furthers this notion stating CSs are "mutual attempts of two interlocutors to agree on a meaning in situations where requisite meaning structures do not seem to be shared" (1980: 419 cited in Smith, 2003: 32). For this reason, it can be said that making second language learners aware of the communication strategies that can be used to overcome gaps in their linguistic knowledge can be valuable in developing effective foreign or second language communicative competence where communicating effectively in the target language does not require accuracy, but in beneficial forms CSs may offer learners comfort when taking risks to meet communication ends where linguistic knowledge is absent.

For most second language learners, to communicate in the target language is of primary importance and takes precedence over reading and writing. Consequently, it is because of this desire to communicate effectively in the target language context, that language learners and teachers focus their attention on CSs. According to Thorne (2000), it is within a community of practice or particular context that interlocutors share meaning through interaction whereby the speakers and listeners utilise their schema or background knowledge to understand one another. This, in turn, offers them the ability to, within the context, understand the intended message independently of what Thorne (2000: 229) describes as "universally distributed linguistic competence". Additionally, Rommetveit (1974, cited in Thorne, 2000: 230) states, "Communication is a co-constructed social process and not an act of simple transmission". This corroborates with sociocultural theories espoused by Vygotsky (1978) together with social constructivism and social interactionist theories whereby the interpretation of second language interaction is co-constructed and language learning does not happen in isolation but within social activity (Lantolf, 2000).

Dörnyei and Scott (1997), in a review of communication strategies in L2 (second language) communication, identify the main taxonomies, which represent the most notable definitions of CSs in face-to-face contexts, which contribute to the negotiation of meaning and sociocultural views of SLA. They emphasise that, among the varying taxonomies, there are ambiguous and, in some instances, contestable definitions resulting in a misrepresentation of the notion of CSs in research. Therefore, Dörnyei and Scott present a comprehensive list of CSs derived from nine taxonomies. However, because of the nature of the present context whereby it is devoid of non-verbal cues, the inventory of CSs was adapted and reduced for the purpose of this short study, thus providing a framework for data analysis. The categories can be found in Table 2.1 which includes definitions and examples.

Strategy	Definition
Message abandonment	Leaving a message left unfinished
Restructuring and self-repair	Making self-initiated corrections; Abandoning the execution of a verbal plan because of language difficulties, then communicating the intended message to an alternative plan
Other repair	Correcting interlocutor's speech
Use of fillers	e.g., mmm, ahhh, okay, you know. To gain time in order to keep the communication channel open and maintain discourse in times of difficulty.
Self-repetition	Repeating an utterance immediately after it was said
Repeating interlocutor's utterance	Repeating what the interlocutor said to gain time.
Expressing non-understanding	Expressing verbal uncertainty when not understanding the interlocutor's utterance.
Clarification request	When the speaker is unsure of what the interlocutor said then asks for the utterance to be repeated or paraphrased. i.e., What did you say? What do you mean?
Interpretive summary	Extended paraphrase of the interlocutor's message to check that the speaker has understood correctly.
Use of similar-sounding words	Compensating for a lexical item the speaker is unsure of which sounds similar to the target item

Table 2.1. Interactional communication strategies from nine taxonomies (Adapted from Dörnyei and Scott, 1997).

Few studies have been conducted in terms of CMC contexts and communication strategies. However, what has been uncovered is that they bring with them a different perspective in the construction of meaning during interaction primarily because of the absence of paralinguistic signals which Epp et al., (2010) assert is one of its benefits in educational environments. Researchers report that such contexts can benefit the development of the second language learning process, thus reflecting the notion of second language acquisition theories (Lin and Fang, 2010; Peterson, 2006; Peterson, 2009; Warschauer, 1996). Lin and Fang's (2010) evaluation of learner perceptions highlighted that language learners who usually experience difficulty communicating in traditional classroom settings, were substantially less stressed and frustrated when following instructions and communicating in the CMC environment. This case study further stressed the importance of the instruction of communication strategies for those with limited linguistic abilities to repair communication gaps because moments of frustration did occur when communication breakdown was experienced. Whilst the results did not show significantly different signs of learning occurring in the CMC environment compared to traditional classroom settings, Peterson's (2009) study, in contrast, found promising results. He states that the notions of sociocultural accounts of language development were in fact present throughout the research. It was found that communication strategies concomitant to collaboration in face-to-face and CMC environments were frequently employed. Consequently, because of the strategies used within the tasks carried out, data showed that participants demonstrated sustained focus for the entirety of the session. An increased use of CSs over a period of time was highlighted, which appeared conducive to the creation of a supportive environment and the successful development of an effective community of practice. This, in turn, is believed to facilitate increased target language communication and an improvement in effective strategic competence (Foster and Ohta, 2005; Peterson, 2009).

2.6. *General summary*

A selection of contemporary studies on education and language learning in CMC contexts were highlighted, in particular learning in virtual worlds, outlining both the affordances and potential drawbacks. This was followed by a summary of communication strategies that occur in second language use with emphasis on their use in CMC contexts. This case study analyses Synchronous CMC (SCMC) using Second Life and attempts to present validating findings concerning the participants' use of communication in this immersive virtual world with the aim of reporting results that can contribute to the current body of research and raise an awareness of the affordances of voice and text activated SCMC contexts for second language learners and educators.

Chapter 3: Methodology

3.1. *Research questions*

Based on the literature review above, which discussed the affordances of educational MUVEs and their apparent drawbacks for education, the research questions, as previously noted in section 1.3, which serve the purpose of shaping this study in order to add to the current literature in this area, are as follows:

1. Out of the selected communication strategies, which do the participants employ most during meaning-focused interaction in Second Life?

2. What significant themes emerge from analysis of communication strategy use during the Second Life session?

3. How is Second Life used for efficient conversational management during group discussion when para-linguistic communication strategies are limited?

3.2. *Data collection*

To answer the research questions, data was analysed and interpreted through a descriptive and constructivist lens with an emphasis on explorative qualitative analysis "to understand the multiple social constructions of meaning and knowledge" (Robson, 2002: 27). This methodology was chosen because the study was not set in a "contrived situation for research purposes" (Punch, 2009: 117), but within a naturalistic setting. Moreover, it focuses on uncovering unanticipated findings and measurement of the participants' communication strategies in Second Life. Drawing from Robson, this approach allows the researcher "[t]o find out what is happening, to seek new insights, to ask questions, to assess the phenomena in a new light and to generate ideas and hypotheses for future research" (2002: 59).

The qualitative data was collected using observation notes and recordings from participants' conversations in two SL sessions which were transcribed and prepared for in-depth analysis. Additionally, a course blog acted as a meeting point for the students to find out about course news, lessons and feedback, and also encouraged them to share their thoughts and opinions about their sessions in SL together with a space for collaboration and further discussion. This open platform, in turn, ensured an environment devoid of researcher presence, for data to emerge naturally thereby strengthening internal validity. To achieve a deeper investigation into the dimensions of student engagement, thematic analysis was utilised to "track the objectives of the discourse and the description of the process of meaning negotiation among participants" (Bower and Hedberg, 2010 cited in Yang, 2011). Robson asserts such importance in qualitative research stating that "language has such a role in social life, the study of it provides the key to understanding our social functioning [...] it is not only the substance of what is said [which forms the basis for conversational analysis] that is important, but the styles and strategies of language users – *how* they say things." (Robson, 2002: 365 emphasis added).

By employing an exploratory case study, it was possible to use a variety of methods to contribute to more holistic interpretations offering stronger, more validating and understandable results (Yin, 2003). While this looked to provide interesting patterns in the use of SL in facilitating the learning of a foreign language, it was understood that it would not be possible to arrive at generalisations (Stake, 1995). What was important for the constructive nature of this study was to record an objective account of what was happening in the development of the case study through the construction of knowledge between the participants whilst “simultaneously examin[ing] its meaning” (Stake, 1995: 77). To that end, my presence as a researcher was controlled in order to have very little contact with the participants during session recordings. Conducting research in SL provided the benefits of observing and recording the participants’ behaviours and language use without causing disruptions through researcher presence, as commonly experienced in observational studies within traditional class-room settings.

Implementing this method of inquiry allowed the researcher to “discern ongoing behaviour as it occurs ... and make appropriate notes about salient features” (Bailey, 1994: 243 cited in Cohen et al., 2006: 260) which would be difficult to obtain in other forms of data collection. Cohen et al. (2006: 260) point out that the potential exists for observational data collection techniques to evoke an element of bias. However, it is emphasised that, whilst bias can be present within the anti-positivist stance in the current study – that is, “the social world can only be understood by occupying the frame of reference of the participant in action” (Williams, 1998: 3) – “the interest [must be] in a subjective, relativistic social world rather than an absolutist, external reality" (Morgan, 1979 cited in Cohen et al., 2006: 8). Thus, ensuring a rich and deep insight into the particular phenomenon is of prime importance during the collection, interpretation and analysis of data.

3.3. Data coding and analysis

According to Foster and Ohta (2005), Ellis (1999), Polio and Gass (1997), and Schachter and Gass (1996) agree "for reliability and generalizability of research findings, the coding of categories is absolutely critical, as is the ability of researchers to apply the categories used in previous research" (Foster and Ohta, 2005: 410). In order to do this, the SL session transcripts were initially analysed according to the communication strategies outlined in Table 2.1 (Chapter 2), thereby coding participants' language use into communication strategy categories, which Robson (2002: 477) terms "first-level coding". This offers a descriptive account of strategy use before evaluating the occurrences through thematic discourse analysis or "second-level coding", thus, providing a larger picture of research evidence (Scott and Morrison, 2006: 33).

There were two sessions. The Session One transcript provided some interesting findings, offering a substantial amount of data to help answer the research questions. Whilst the current study ran for only a month and included only two SL sessions, it was felt that analysing both sessions within such a close time frame might not provide strong comparative results. Therefore, only Session One was chosen for analysis in an attempt to obtain a rich insight into language use and behaviour during the session. The advantage of using the first group session for analysis is that it can offer EFL practitioners who have little or no experience of using SL the knowledge of whether using it for teaching is a viable option on a short term basis. In addition, using only one session allowed for a more detailed and rich analysis of data.

The session transcript was examined primarily with manual discourse analysis which was supported by screen capture recordings of the full session – using *Camtasia* software – together with learner feedback posted on the course blog and an unstructured short focus group session. This was done to highlight the learners' perceptions of their experiences and took place immediately after the meeting because their opinions about learning in SL would then be most valid. In addition, implementing a focus group ensured that all members of the group could offer opinions without the need to organise individual interviews; thus eliminating the possibility of non-attendance. It is important that, "participants are empowered and able to make comments in their own words, while being stimulated by thoughts and comments or others in the group." (Robson, 2002: 285).

The session transcript was initially coded using the selected strategies from second language acquisition (SLA) literature outlined in Table 2.1. The strategies were coded within the transcript and the number of occurrences of each strategy was then calculated. This coded data formed the body of findings for qualitative data analysis with an aim to achieve a deeper understanding of the participants' strategy use and how the strategies are used during interactions (Silverman, 2001).

The session recordings were viewed on several occasions, highlighting each strategy chosen for analysis because the nuances of intonation, pauses and movement within the session can be overlooked when coding the transcript alone. This process retrieved themes, topic control, turn taking and length of turns and cues for the in-depth analysis described in the following chapter. To add to the data available, the voice and text contributions made by each participant were calculated; thus providing additional information on the significant themes emerging throughout the session.

3.4. Ethics in an online environment

> *As researchers venture into excavate virtual worlds, it seems reasonable to take a moment to think about what these worlds represent and how we can approach them most suitably. Virtual worlds also propose an interesting ethical challenge since they, through simulation of space, resemble offline environments more than other online environments.* (Rosenburg, 2010: 23)

Taking Rosenburg's views into consideration, it is important to ensure participants are reminded of their privacy rights, particularly as this immersive environment presents the illusion that the data produced is private. Therefore, for the purpose of this study it was imperative that both researcher and participants understood that this is not the case and that to take part in this online study raises the possibility that, whilst any information they share is protected by the researcher, there is always the potential it is stored permanently among a vast amount of data within the online service. To highlight such issues, informed consent was a requirement for the data provided to be recorded and used for research purposes, which

Cohen et al. affirm is the "[participants] right to freedom and self determination" and thus "places some of the responsibility on the participant should anything go wrong in the research" (2006: 52). Furthermore, the participants were reminded of their right to withdraw at any time during the research and that if they were to do so, efforts would be made by the researcher to delete all information they provided, whether it was from participant observations, conversations, focus groups or questionnaires (Robson, 2002). The participants were also assured that their identity would not be disclosed within the documentation of research findings and if interested, they would be issued with a copy of the report upon request.

3.5. Research participants and context

This study comprised a purposive sample and out of thirty-two applicants nine were initially chosen to participate in a pilot online course – which the present case study was integrated with. The participants were drawn from two ability levels – upper intermediate and advanced levels of English. Whilst these levels were not tested, all participants expressed a competent ability in English to fit the requirements of the current study. Furthermore, participants were chosen based on their geographic location with the aim of gathering EFL learners from diverse cultural backgrounds but, because of the synchronous context of SL and the varying time zones in which both participants and myself were located, it was possible for distance to hinder smooth communication (Kingsley and Wankel, 2009). Therefore, it was essential that all successful participants could offer the time, computer capacity to install the SL client software and a fast internet connection required to function smoothly as a whole group within this virtual environment.

While all participants expressed a desire to take part in the study, prior to the pilot online course commencing, five subsequently withdrew because of both personal and unanticipated technological and time difference problems. This left only three native Chinese speakers and one native German speaker, and only three EFL learner participants and the EFL teacher participant agreed to attend both SL sessions. Despite this, those who did participate fulfilled the appropriate criteria on a number of levels – no participant had any experience in socialising or learning in SL. Furthermore, whilst two of the participants were from China, they were located in two different prefectures and had no knowledge of one another before the study commenced. While the diverse cultural differences were reduced, the final sample still comprised three different nationalities, thus offering the potential for a variety of socio-cultural perspectives during task discussions.

Table 3.1 summarises the participants' English abilities, geographic information, age, gender and SL experience, as taken from a pre-course application questionnaire (see Appendix 1). The participants who attended the SL sessions did so voluntarily on the basis of the requirements of the pilot online EFL course and importantly, all provided written consent for the data to be used for the purpose of this current study.

Name	Age	Gender	English level	Location	Second Life experience
Teacher	31	M	Native speaker	Scotland	4 months
Student 1	41	F	Advanced	Germany	None
Student 2	22	F	Advanced	China	None
Student 3	25	M	Upper intermediate	China	None
Student 4	24	M	Upper intermediate	China	None

Table 3.1. Research participants

The project ran for one month in June 2011 which included an initial orientation session for each participant; following this, the group met together on the last two Saturdays that month. Each session in SL took place on the University of Edinburgh sim, *Vue* (Virtual University of Edinburgh) – "an educational and research institute bringing together all those using virtual worlds for teaching, research and outreach" (Morse et al., 2009: 187).

While *Vue* provides a variety of areas from which to conduct research studies or lessons on 'virtual' ground level, the first session took place, for the full duration, in a cloud in the sky (see Figure 1). The reason for using this space for the first task was that it offered the participants a safe and controlled environment free from the possibility of eavesdroppers and a reduced chance of uninvited SL residents interrupting the session. It could be argued that unplanned instances arising could potentially aid the authentic conversational experience and the chance for the learners to interact with native target language speakers or other English language learners. However, for ethical reasons, considering the session was being recorded, it was felt that such occurrences could contaminate the research. Secondly, because of potential bandwidth constraints, meeting in areas where there was an array of animated objects, meant that computer lag threatened the flow of conversation. Therefore, conducting the session in an area free from complex objects reduced the chance of the participants' SL viewers crashing and smooth communication throughout was ensured. One participant expressed her gratitude regarding the care taken over the location of the sessions in course feedback stating, "At the moment I can say I loved the safe environment, where we all talked. It was easy to interact, because you know who you dealt with and your support to interact helped a lot" (S1, see Appendix 4).

Image 3.1. Vue cloud – SL classroom

As noted in the literature review, it was suggested that induction sessions are necessary to ease the learners into the new environment to avoid technological frustrations and ensure learners and instructors can enjoy the virtual environment's educational experience to its fullest extent. Therefore, participants met individually for a short briefing session several days prior to the scheduled group meeting. During this session the participants were guided through the basics of functioning in SL, learning how to move and control the avatar, i.e. walking, sitting, flying, taking pictures, teleporting, using voice and adjusting their interlocutor avatar's volume.

The participants were then invited to take part in two sessions, which lasted approximately one hour and twenty minutes each. The first was held for its full duration in the cloud and the other was held in the cloud for the majority of the time but also in an English speaking location, chosen by one of the participants, for a fifteen-minute exploration task with the assistance of the teacher and in the presence of the researcher. Both sessions were completed as a whole group, using pre-designed tasks appropriate to their SL experience, which are explained in more detail in the following section.

3.6. *Pedagogy and social constructivist connections*

The current study's tasks considered the interactional potentials, which correspond to Long's reformulation of the *Interactionist* hypothesis (1996) that "taking part in interaction can facilitate second language development." (Mackey, 1999: 565 cited in Mitchell and Myles, 2004: 173). In addition, the task design utilised echoed Vygotsky's zone of proximal development theory – that through collaborations with those more able, the learner will be "inducted into a shared understanding [...] until eventually they appropriate new knowledge or skills into their own individual consciousness" (Mitchell and Myles, 2004: 195). What is more, the task design was developed from social constructivist principles, which Mikropoulus and Natsis assert "is the theoretical approach the majority of EVEs [Educational Virtual Environments] is based on" (2011: 771). They offer a clearer perspective of social constructivism and outline the seven main principles according to Jonassen (1994), which are as follows:

1. Provide multiple representations of reality – avoiding oversimplification of instruction by representing the natural complexity of the world
2. Focus on knowledge construction not reproduction
3. Present authentic tasks (contextualising rather than abstracting instruction)
4. Provide real world, case based learning environments, rather than pre-determined instructional sequences
5. Foster reflective practice
6. Enable context, and content, dependent knowledge construction
7. Support collaborative construction of knowledge through social negotiation, not competition among learners for recognition

(Cited in Mikropoulos and Natsis, 2011: 772)

Johnassen (1994) asserts that while these principles detail social constructivist learning, they only present the grounding of such an approach and it is not necessary for *all* principles to be present for a lesson to be socially constructivist in nature. They merely provide a framework on which to base pedagogy (Mikropoulos and Natsis, 2011).

To offer further insight, social constructivist views of teaching have also been linked to the notion of 'connectivism' which "accommodates both transmission approaches to teaching and learning and social constructivist views of teaching and learning that accord with web 2.0 dialogue building and social networking tools" (Senior, 2010: 137). Therefore, because the course in which the participants belonged was based on social constructivist principles, the task implemented for this study was developed on this notion. It was also loosely based on a multi-dimensional framework described by Kucer and Silva (2006) in that it is designed around cognitive, linguistic, sociocultural and developmental perspectives and aims to ensure a structure to promote meaningful learning and meet learning goals (Vygotsky, 1978; Wenger et al., 2009). The authenticity of the task and a learner-centred approach is crucial to the theory behind the present task design, with a primary aim to "encourage the sharing of ideas between teacher and students and support one another towards the collaboration of new ideas and shared knowledge to create new understandings" (Pegrum, 2009: 27). Therefore, this perspective "focuses on learning as a social process wherein students acquire knowledge through proactive interaction with significant others" (Snowman and Biehler, 2000 cited in Gu et al., 2009: 161).

Session One comprised three individual relationship-building activities designed to elicit personal opinions about a variety of topics, which emerged through conversation, while at the same time utilising some of the affordances and artefacts particular to the virtual space. While this lesson design does not display the more sophisticated task types possible in SL, the task chosen is suitable for the learners' level of experience in SL, allowing them to acclimatise to the new environment. Salmon affirms this, stating that before implementing complex virtual environment exploiting affordances, it is important for the teacher or e-moderator "to create a climate that will strongly enhance the well-being of the online group, based on respect and support for each other [...] In this way, intrinsic motivators will gradually emerge, and learning will be promoted" (2011: 36).

Chapter 4: Presentation of findings

4.1. *Participation and communication strategy use*

From coding the data for communication strategy use, this section presents an answer to research question 1: *Out of the selected communication strategies, which do the participants employ most during meaning-focused interaction in Second Life?*

First, the transcript data was examined to identify the communication strategies (CSs) used by each participant. The analysis of the transcripts indicates that out of the selected communication strategies for analysis, there was a high occurrence of timesaving devices, self-repair and self-repetition used by each participant with very little variance between them. Table 4.1 shows a breakdown of the CS frequency retrieved from Session One, which was selected for qualitative analysis, as discussed below.

Communication strategies	T	S1	S2	S3
Turns/cues	253 (37%)	156 (23%)	141 (21%)	123 (18%)
Fillers	45	99	177	134
Message abandonment	3	5	2	2
Restructuring and self-repair	4	13	23	9
Other repair	2	0	0	0
Repeating interlocutor's utterance	5	0	3	2
Self-repetition	13	16	44	20
Expressing non understanding	2	1	1	2
Clarification request	4	3	3	4
Interpretive summary	7	2	7	3
Use of similar-sounding words	0	1	1	2

Table 4.1. Frequency and comparison of conversational strategy use during SL Session One.

4.2. *Emerging themes uncovered by strategy use*

Analysis of the transcript indicated the predominant behavioural themes present from examining individuals' communication strategy use were *power relations*, *politeness for a desire to develop and sustain interpersonal relationships,* and *risk taking* which are discussed in detail in the following section. Thus offering an answer to research question 2: *What significant themes emerge from analysis of communication strategy use during the Second Life session?*

It can be inferred that these particular themes emerged partly because this was the first group session for the learners. Whilst there are no comparisons to be made with regards to later sessions in this analysis of data, the behaviour communicated by the participants may contribute to the learners' beliefs on instruction based on their cultural background. A possible explanation for this, according to Deutschman and Panichi is that the participants are "unsure of their roles in the group and leave the control to the teacher, who therefore has to play a more central role in managing the conversation" (2011: 322). However, these findings contribute to and support research on communication strategy use in SCMC virtual environments.

4.2.1. Conversation facilitation and topic control

From a top-down perspective, it is clear from the analysis of the data that the session was learner-centred with an emphasis on the construction of knowledge – a more meaning-focused session as opposed to form-focused, thus offering learners more freedom for expression and a greater opportunity for authentic conversational interactions.

However, taking a closer look at the number of turns the teacher takes (37%) in relation to the number of turns the three learners collectively take (62%) shows it to be heavily teacher-centred (see Figure 4.1). Despite this, it can be argued that this level of interaction on the teacher's part matches the requirement for ensuring both the smooth flow of conversation and the need to create a welcoming atmosphere to foster the emergence of the new community, offering all members the opportunity to share their opinions and anecdotes (Wenger et al., 2009). It is, therefore, important to note that the lengths of the teacher's cues remained short and also choice of topic throughout the discussion was not planned but co-constructed by the participants vocally or by text chat, which, in turn, elicited active authentic conversational participation. An example of this emerged in lines 1, 2, 5 and 6 within the excerpt below.

In the following examples from the transcript, the topic of relevance is displayed in bold and the symbols, '/' and '//' denote the length of a pause. Where there is '(.)' this defines a noticeable but very short pause and any text in italics presents turns taken in text chat.

Excerpt 1

S3: ah today, I (.) I (.) tshhh (drawing a breath through his teeth) **s... I go to a cinema to see em a movie ... tshh... ahh Pirates of Caribbean.**

S2: Ah excellent!

T: great. / have you all seen the other eh Pirates of the Caribbean movies?

S2: yes

S3: ah 1, 2, 3, 4. I think, all of them

S2: yes (.) yes me too all of them

T: great what, what do you think's the best one? /

(This topic continues for a further 18 lines)

After a number of turns by each participant (S1, 2 and 3), and based on S3's topic prompt the teacher (T) takes the lead to move the conversation forward, initiating the beginning of a new topic:

Excerpt 2

S3: so eh... **this afternoon I saw the 3D. 3D eh...**
version
movie (.) / It is perfect, I think.

S2: me too

T: ah I see. **What does everyone think about 3D in the**
cinema? //Do you think it's good to have 3D in the
cinema?

T: [text chat] *what do you think about 3D in the cinema?*

S2: I don't think so, mmm because in my city 3D technology is
poor so (.) so I can't see no difference between 2D and 3D emmm...

The teacher continues to take control of the conversation throughout the session apart from one occasion when S2 makes an attempt to take 'topic control'. However, despite the student's efforts to change the subject whilst remaining responsive, the teacher bypasses the suggestion in order to meet his own ends:

Excerpt 3

S2: How about you T? What kind of music do you like?

T: [in a very enthusiastic tone] I loooove a variety of music. I am obsessed with music. I always listen to different... different styles, genres of music. I think music is my life. Hehehe...

S2: me too me too... so can you tell me eh... what are the eh eh different kind's of music styles, like em blues, jazz. But, I don't know what they are difference. I have to know about it even though I love musics so much. //

At this point, to assume control, the teacher offers, according to Jupp, a "dis-preferred response" (2006: 43 cited in Bax, 2011: 79), presenting the first communication breakdown in the session as the teacher's response diverges from the expected response (Hutchby, 2001):

T: I think it's nice to listen to lots of different styles and varieties of music //

The teacher then proposes an alternative course of action, as presented in the following line:

T: Do any of you play a musical instrument?

This form of interaction is viewed as important within conversational analysis as it displays useful underlying messages (Bax, 2011). It can be interpreted that the teacher wants to avoid direct attention within conversation either to reduce the length of his cues or talking time or keep focused on what the *learners* have to say, always remaining focused on his course of action.

Throughout the session, the teacher adopts a conversational style of speech, where interactions appear social and non-instructive or, as one participant described in course feedback, as 'non-schooly'. The observations also convey this tone through the relaxed manner of speech and intonations, making him appear friendly, interested and personable; thus developing a rapport with the learners. Despite this, the teacher's turn-taking, topic redirecting and the number of questions initiated, implicitly demonstrates the presence of hierarchical behaviour, which according to Salmon (2011) is broken down considerably within SL-based lessons, as noted in the literature review. That said, this level of control could be seen to display his role as e-moderator rather than simply 'joining in with discussion'; thus highlighting the importance of developing and nurturing socialisation through positive reinforcement and taking interest in each individual learner (Salmon, 2011).

A closer look at the data presents notable findings on teacher participation. Whilst the transcript presents the teacher in an authoritative light in his approach to asking questions, e.g., in Excerpt 2, "What does everyone think about 3D in the cinema? // Do you think it's good to have 3D in the cinema?" and, in Excerpt 3, "Do any of you play a musical instrument?" The video observations on the other hand show that the teacher only asked questions when long pauses were present. Therefore, the teacher only contributed to the session where signs of communication breakdown were showing.

Whilst this may not demonstrate natural social interactions, it does ensure all learners feel comfortable and are welcomed to participate equally; thus they are encouraged to take risks in their output of the target language. Salmon affirms this by stating, "Online group work will not in itself create the social interaction. Sensitive and appropriate learning design and the e-moderator's intervention enable the socialisation for learning to occur" (2011: 36).

The learners do not appear to be affected or particularly aware of this power relation and indirect topic control and thus willingly co-operate within conversations, often mirroring the supportive role the teacher frequently demonstrates.

4.3. Risk taking

After the transcript was analysed and coded for CS use based on Table 2.1 in Chapter 2, the data displayed some interesting findings in terms of turn taking and organised interaction as discussed above. However, there appeared to be limited evidence of strategies as can be seen from Table 4.1, in particular, *other repair* – i.e., correcting interlocutors utterance, *message abandonment, repeating interlocutors utterance* and the *use of similar sounding words.*

Whilst it is noted that the teacher displayed signs of instructive teacher behaviour, there were very few instances where he corrected or repaired the learners' linguistic errors which may have had a positive impact on risk taking among the learners.

In terms of risk taking, from the limited use of the strategies, such as *the use of similar-sounding words,* it could be inferred that the participants did not make any attempt to take risks in their output. Conversely, the learners also did not show many cases of abandoning messages and when they did show signs of possible message abandonment, they reviewed their utterance and then took the opportunity to rephrase it or start again, thus successfully meeting communication ends. For example, the excerpt below – an interaction between the teacher (T), Student 1 (S1) and Student 2 (S2) at the beginning of the session – presents such an occurrence. However feedback, reinforcement and scaffolding (lines 9, 13, 14, 17, 18, 25, 26, and 29) from the teacher and S1, resulted in S2 achieving a desired outcome.

This instance also presents a clear case of sociocultural communication with a greater need for negotiation of meaning, conversational adjustment and speech modification, since the participants have no shared cultural background, the topic in this case being popular music among the older generation in China. With very little knowledge or shared understanding, S2 struggles to describe the music to the other group members:

Excerpt 4

T: Cos S1 was saying that they have em music for older like older people in Germany, for an older sound and is there something similar in China? /

S2: yes yes em em mmm now it is eh the ah mmm you know lot's of ahh retired people the old people they they like to ah ah take a walk and em and dance with people ah ah mmm mmm mm each night when you go out you can see lot's of old people ahh get together in in our centre square and dance when mmm that kind of mmm I mean mmm ahh typical music that eh (.) appea... appealing to them

As opposed to simply answering 'yes' or a giving a similar short, direct answer to the teacher's question, S2 takes a risk to try to verbally 'paint a picture'.

T: Ah I see

Showing presence at this stage encourages S2 to continue.

S2: I don't know what ah type of music. It's mm just not so popular for young people eh but they like it eh and they dance eh eh dance with it each night. Do you can see old people dance.

T: What style of dancing?

S1 they dance in open space? /

S2: eh I don't know how what the name of that dance you know just eh eh couple ehh sorry hahahah I don't know ehhh /

T: I think S1 was asking [S2: mmhhmm] do they do they dance in open space? So can you see them in a public space?

S2: yes yes yes yes yes In a public space and eh anyone em can join them if eh if they like if they would like to. //

T: [wrote in the local chat] – ***cool I want to see it.***

At this stage, S2 is possibly aware that her explanation is not enough to truly provide an accurate description of the music and dancing, and therefore finds a solution by informing the group members that she will use her blog to show them in words and image what she was trying to portray.

S2: yes yes of course em also I don't know how to name it in English maybe maybe next time I'll introduce introduce the traditional Chinese dance in my blog okay? Hahaha hahahaaa

S1: [wrote in local text chat] ***wow that's a real get together then***

T: I will look forward to that // sounds great ye heheh

S2: also I'll introduce mmm ahh what it ehh about introduce the popular music in China… next time hmhmhmhehe

S1: Excellent / ye sounds great.

The desire to construct meaning on this occasion interestingly presented signs of learner autonomy. Without taking direction from the teacher, the learners were willing to express themselves through alternative means, such as the using the course blog for further explanation.

Additionally, another occasion in the session revealed – from observation – that S3 also presented interesting signs of risk taking whilst engaging in language production. For approximately forty-five minutes into the session, S3 awaited direction from the teacher for a turn to speak, however fifty-three minutes into the session, marked the point when he began to contribute to the discussion without relying on any prompting from the teacher. In turn, his turns became longer, thus appearing more confident in his language production. This behaviour indicates that he was more comfortable with the environment and his role as a group member. It could also be inferred at this point that the power relations were changing, with the teacher being viewed as an equal participant in the conversation.

4.3.1. *Restructuring and self-repair*

Communication strategy	T	S1	S2	S3
Restructuring and self-repair	4	13	23	9

Table 4.2. Comparison of repair strategies

Another significant finding from the data, in terms of risk taking, was the occurrence of self-repair by all student participants (see Table 4.2). From a close analysis of the interactions, there were only minor occurrences of explicit instances of self-repair. For example, during a long turn by S2, at the end of her utterance she is evidently monitoring her output, corrects it and then acknowledges the error she has made:

Excerpt 5

(6 lines of S2's turn in line one are omitted)

S2: The original movies are **much more cool, is eh (.) eh, much**
cooler sorry hehehehe... grammar mistake.

However, whilst short turns both in voice and in text displayed very few instances of self-repair, the text chat function offered the participants a means of rectifying any possible misunderstandings or to clarify meaning when the utterance, in the speaker's opinion, failed to convey the intended message. The following excerpt presents an example of this, and is another example of monitored output:

Excerpt 6

S3: Young people tend to young people tend to go to the tshhh… the original version and eh some other people just like the (.) eh (.) eh older ones they like to see the translated one movies.

However, S3 found another opening thirty-four lines on, but rather than vocalise the repair and risk the potential of communication breakdown again, he chose to utilise the text chat in an attempt to syntactically modify his previous output, thus confirming his point and making his message clearer:

Excerpt 7

S3: *So young people tend to see the original. I am 25*

However, another turn by the same student later in the session produced the following:

Excerpt 8

S3: … try my best to do that to make everything right but eh

when I off work I ehh not eh try to eh forget **what I done**
what I have done ah in the day night [[evening]] shhhh
(inhaled through his teeth) eh so it well easy my ten..tennis
[[tension]] I will sleep eh well much well in the night.

Interestingly, S3 who displayed more instances of syntactical, phonological and lexical problems than the other student participants utilised fewer cases of self-correction. Whilst it could be argued that his language production could benefit from explicit instances of correction or recasts from the teacher (Ellis et al., 1994), this approach may hinder the flow of conversation and potentially discourage the learner from taking risks, inhibiting his confidence in contributing to further discussion.

4.3.2. *Negotiation of meaning*

However, although they are not directly associated with risk-taking strategies, the instances of negotiation of meaning during this session are just as important as they are valuable to linguistic development and also in line with second language acquisition theory. According to Long, "the role of free conversation is notoriously poor as a context for driving interlanguage development" (1996: 249). However, that is not to say that learning does not occur within such conversational contexts as van Lier argues, "[f]rom all complex phenomena that may occur in interaction, the notion of the negotiation of meaning is highlighted as being indicative of learning processes at work, or at least as a likely candidate for learning opportunities" (2000: 247). For example, an interaction between S1 and S2, whilst engaged in a communication gap task, illustrates an explicit instance of the negotiation of meaning:

<u>Excerpt 9</u>

S2: what does that mean, super dyuper? Doooper... Super duper. [continues to practice]

T: Can you explain that S1?

S1: It's just (.) if something's really really really super, then you say 'super duper' hehe

T: [laughter]

S3: Super duper.

T: I love it!

And that should be compared with the conversational interaction between the teacher and S2:

<u>Excerpt 10</u>

T: what do you like about Pirates of the Caribbean?

S2: eh mmm I just admire captain mmm captain Jack annnmm he eh he always try to be himself and try to mmm seek and enjoy freedom eh it's just like me so I eehh love him a lot .

T: wonderful...

In the first example, a clear instance of negotiation of meaning is present. Whilst the second extract does not explicitly constitute an instance of learning linguistically, that is not to say that S2 is not challenging herself cognitively as she is negotiating her identity, explaining who she is, her position in life and what she strives to be (van Leir, 2000).

This example presents a partial account of the nature of the conversation which developed through the session where the negotiations between interlocutors showed that a personal investment within the information constructed was inherently present throughout.

Together with the numerous instances of seeking clarification and self-correcting, it is through these alterations during negotiated interaction it is realised that, according to Long (1996), "the most valuable way in which input is made more comprehensible" (cited in Foster and Ohta, 2005: 405).

It is through taking risks in the target language output that incomprehensible utterances are produced. This increases the number of instances of the interlocutor's need for meanings to be negotiated. Accordingly, Foster and Ohta state that this occurrence "prompts attention to language forms and precision in phonology, lexis and morphosyntax" (2005: 406). Consequently, second language acquisition is facilitated.

4.4. *Strategies used in text chat*

Research has indicated that the use of text chat in CMC communication allows for more explicit occurrences of 'noticing' as identified in the previous discussion, thereby encouraging the correcting or restructuring of linguistic form (Warschauer, 1997). However, whilst such occurrences took place solely in text-based synchronous CMC (SCMC), in the current study, the use of text chat together with oral communication in SL, presents additional interesting findings in terms of communication strategies and interaction.

Thus it provides possible answers to research question 3: *How is Second Life used for efficient conversational management during group discussion when paralinguistic communication strategies are limited?*

Table 4.3 shows the use of text chat by each participant as a percentage of the overall number of turns taken and compares their usage of text chat in terms of the number of turns.

Communication strategy	**T**	**S1**	**S2**	**S3**
Total text chat use	38 (15% overall turns taken)	51 (33)%	14 (10)%	27 (22)%
Non-vocal turn taking input (Interlocutors contribute to conversation via text chat)	11	16	11	13
Clarification requests	0	2	0	1
Conformation checks/self repetition	5	1	1	4
Fillers	2	9	0	0
Feedback response	19	21	1	8
Repair (self and other)	1	3	1	1
Emoticons (text-based paralinguistic signals)	0	1	0	0

Table 4.3. Use of text chat

The main usage of text chat occurred during the session's first planned activity. The teacher implemented an activity where he presented the beginning of a sentence and elicited completion by the learners. The main purpose of this activity was to make the students comfortable with the communicative functionality of SL using both voice and text during discussion and, most importantly, to keep all the participants focused as a group. This was to avoid any confusion if there are a number of things happening simultaneously (Hockly and Clandfield, 2010). The answers retrieved from the activity provided topics and elicited increased participation, thus providing additional points for conversation.

Besides being used for the task, which interestingly made a significant increase in text chat use within further non-activity based discussion, text chat was effectively used for clarification, paraphrasing or repetition of previous utterances, self or other repair and feedback signals. In terms of fillers, they appeared less frequently in text chat than they did during oral communication. Interestingly, fillers such as, 'wow', 'ok', and an indication of laughter, were employed in text chat interchangeably with voice chat, but more consciously – as can be seen from the excerpt below:

<u>Excerpt 11</u>

S1: so em what would your business be then? //

S3: Foreign trade

T: Ah... foreign trade? /

S1 *ok*

S3: *Foreign trade*

S1: *wow!*

T: What type of things would you trade? //**S3:** I think eh about eh
shoes? Or in electronic product eh and eh

S1: Go for the shoes!! [Laughter]

[S1, S2, S3 & T laugh]

T: ***hahahaha***

S3: China, China is the manufacturing factory of the world you know? Eh most shoes in the world was produced in China.

S2: Yes, many in (place name 1) right?

S1: ***yeah?***

S3: yeah (place name 1) and eh (place name 2)

T: *I take it you like shoes S1?*

Identifiably, this conscious employment of fillers in text chat suggests a requirement to show presence. Utilising text chat in this manner provides an assurance that the interlocutor remains interested and is still present in the current topic of conversation without committing to a longer turn.

Whilst the text chat function provided a platform for corrections and feedback signals, it also provided assistance for organised communication management, where it delivered opportunities to self-select turns and initiate topic nomination, as successfully demonstrated in the following extract. In this example, S2 acknowledges the T's cue in line 5, "work politics" and then takes control, acknowledging his turn. However S2 then smoothly changes conversational direction, picking up on an earlier prompt from the teacher in reply to S1's anecdote about her work life "Ahhh stressful (voice)", and "*Stressful? (Text)*" (6 lines prior to S1's turn in line 1):

<u>Excerpt 12</u>

(3 lines of S1s turn omitted)

S1: departed in four different rooms. Now there's decisions to make. Who sits with whom and who doesn't want to sit with whom sohoho hehe...

S3: ahhhh I see

T: *Work politics*

S3: *I see*

S1: ye very much

S2: About the **work politics,** I really afraid of that. I used to work in a company for three months. I HATE work politics. That's the only thing that make me stressful, so...

S3: *I see*

S2: ... S1, **how do you deal with your stress?**

This approach to conversation management is a strong example of efficient interpersonal communication. S2 is aware of a gap or silence and acts accordingly with the disjunctive marker, "About work politics..." (Wong and Waring, 2010). Before committing to her opinion about 'stress', S2 offers the floor to S1; this is a further example of competent conversational control. According to Wong and Waring, this style of topic shift does not "come easily even for proficient speakers" (2010: 103), but it is "vital to one's interactional competence". Therefore, drawing attention to this form of topic control on the part of the learner can help the teacher to discern behavioural patterns in the learner's speech and acknowledge its importance to efficient conversation management during instances of more form-focused instruction.

4.4.1 Self-repetition

Self-repetition was one of the most frequently used strategies in the session and particularly in oral communication. The data reveals that self-repetition was used in an effort to highlight or accent the point the speaker intends to put forward. This strategy could also be perceived to be a filler to gain time, to review and re-structure the intended utterance; whereas in text chat, self-repetition was used to clarify or confirm salient points ensuring that the interlocutor receives the correct message in instances where there may have been pronunciation or voice quality problems. For example, the following interaction between S2 and S3 provides an example of the speakers employing both modalities, restructuring (vocally) and topic emphasis (text). Also, using text in this way concludes S3's turn thus offering an opening to the group to contribute to the conversation:

Excerpt 13

1 **S2:** yeah what is your interest?

2 **S3:** My interest is eh contact with people and **eh learning eh**

from tshhh ah **learning** from a other **peoples** eh other foreign
peoples //
S3: ***My interest***

4.5. *Strategies and politeness*

Politeness	T	S1	S2	S3
Overall politeness **(i.e. niceties – greetings, apologies, farewells)**	69	19	18	14
Positive reinforcement	60	17	13	9

Table 4.4 Comparison of politeness

An interesting finding is the number of supportive feedback responses each participant contributes to the discussions (see Table 4.4) which is strong evidence of a need to develop and sustain collaborative interpersonal relationships. This supports the nature of the meaning-focused task in that it was based on individuals' real lives in an attempt to bring the group closer together as a community of practice.

Excerpt 11 above also highlights the presence of strategy used for politeness, which is embedded within text chat. Its use by the listener presents a respect for the speaker using the voice function, thus eliminating any vocal interference or intrusive overlap. Text chat presents a platform where group members can offer input without fear of causing confusion, cutting off the speaker mid-utterance, or impairing the flow of the speaker's turn, thus ensuring a smoothly managed conversation. Additionally, given the absence of paralinguistic signals which essentially provide important cues for turn allocation and ensure quieter members of the conversation are still included – in particular gaze and body language – text chat provided an alternative for such subtle change in conversational direction or as a means to include the quieter members. Line 16 in Excerpt 11, "T: *I take it you like shoes, S1?*" highlights a requirement to include the listeners through subtle humour. However, this turn taken by the teacher also presents a disruption between adjacency pairs known as 'multi-threading' or "multiple simultaneous topics" (Anderson et al., 2010) which commonly occur in Multi-User Dimensions (MUD) discourse. This occurrence of 'multi-threading' did not show any breakdown of conversation which Mckinlay et al. (1993 cited in Anderson et al., 2010) asserts can inhibit the co-ordination of CMC communication. Despite this, Condon and Cech affirm "participants look for means to exploit the characteristics of different systems to accomplish communication means, including turn-taking, more efficiently" (2001 cited in Anderson et al., 2010: 16), which corresponds to the particular instance in the above excerpt.

This presence of politeness between interlocutors, from culturally diverse backgrounds, assumes the emergence of sociocultural patterns. An illustrative example of this can be seen in the following interaction taken from the beginning of the session, when an attempt at construction of meaning presented some conversational breakdown when S1 attempted to explain to the other group members a definition of 'Schlager' music.

S2 misunderstood S1's utterance (lines 2 – 4) but continued her line of action, coming across as direct – syntactically and in intonation – despite the fact that she was trying to flatter S1 (line 6), "Of course! You said it's for OLD people". Line 8 presents an addition to her comment. She restructured the intended message, taking the edge off the directness of her previous comment using a complimentary adjective – "beautiful" – coupled with soft laughter, which again bears no relevance to the conversation. In return, S1's approach to politeness in her response, aiming to rectify any misunderstandings, contained 'hedging', e.g., *I think* – a strategy which is viewed by analysts as "modifying the truth value of the whole proposition or as avoiding full commitment to the content expressed" (Shengming, 2009: 30). Dorenyei and Scott refer to such instances of speech as 'indirect strategies' which they state "do not provide alternative meaning structures, but rather facilitate the conveyance of meaning indirectly by creating the conditions for achieving mutual understanding; preventing breakdowns and keeping the communication channel open" (1997: 198). However S2 swiftly cut herself out of the conversation firmly in line 13. Whilst she also employed politeness in the response, "OKAY, okay, sorry I don't know about THAT" is somewhat negative. This was conveyed in her intonation and ended any further contributions to the topic of conversation. S1's subsequent turn in line 14, however, softened the directness presented by S2 through interspersing laughter around the utterances, taking any edge off possible tension which, in turn, can also be viewed as a means to overcome paralinguistic absence. It also expressed her need to sustain or ensure supportive relationships with the group members.

Excerpt 14

T: Schlager?

S1: so it's like em // le [[the]] people like to listen to or dance to. So, if you're havin' a party, it can be really nice, but most of the times I don't like it hehehehehe...

T: ahhhh, I see.

S2: Of course! You said it's for OLD people.

T: hahaha

S2: Yeye and beautiful. Of course you won't like it hahaha

S1: I (.) I know people my age who LOVE Schlager so umm it's not really an age thing, but a matter of taste **I think hehehehe...**

S2: OKAY okay, sorry I don't know about THAT.

S1: [laughing] that's all right [laughing]

This finding supports Peterson's finding that there was a high frequency of positive politeness throughout his study which he asserts "reflected the success of such strategies in establishing and maintaining collaborative interpersonal relationships" (2010:

287). These findings also relate to Sherblom et al.'s study which showed that, whilst there were communicative challenges, SL is effective in "facilitating the process of getting to know people [...] and in fostering a professional orientation to group participation, collaboration and brainstorming" (2009: 42).

Chapter 5: Discussion

5.1. Introduction

The results presented in Chapter 4 suggest that when there is a need or requirement to communicate, interlocutors adjust their strategies to the environment in which they are interacting and the group members with whom they are engaged, in this case especially so since the pedagogical approach was based on sociocultural and social-constructivism perspectives. The exploration of linguistic behaviour and how it affects the interaction between the learners assumes that it is through this socialisation and interaction that learning occurs. This notion of learning is supported by views on language learning and development expressed by, amongst others, van Lier (2000), Wenger et al. (2009), and Vygotsky (1978). According to Mitchel and Myles (2004):

> *[C]urrent ethnographies of second language communication and of second language socialisation offer a great deal of evidence about how learning context, and the learners evolving style of engagement with it, may affect the rate of second language learning. The patterning of learning opportunities, through communities of practice with structured and sometimes very unequal power relationships, has been invoked to explain learners' differential success even where motivation is high.* (2004: 255)

5.2. *Discussion and implications*

The analysis of the communication strategies employed shows that the way in which they were utilised suggests language development in tandem with sociocultural principles. For instance, the data shows that the strategies the participants employed, established from sociocultural literature, were often those of politeness, particularly from the Chinese participants where social etiquette is embedded in their language and culture. This places importance on efficiently managed communication and development of valuable interpersonal skills. However, according to Senior, polite attitudes are those of "establishing rapport, which can be achieved with relatively simple interpersonal and class management behaviours that in no way undermine their authority, [is] something that all teachers should seek with their classes." (2010: 141).

The high level of politeness observed throughout the session shares a relationship with the early stages of socialisation and developing relationships with group members. In addition, the results also show that the explicitly polite occurrences of turn taking relate to the absence of paralinguistic signals. In order to signal involvement, remain active in discussion, and engage in cooperative behaviour, whilst maintaining "standard conventions of turn-taking logical sequence and time ordering" (Crystal, 2006: 176) the learners adapted to the environment and met communication needs by utilising text, thereby showing respect to the speaker. "Plainly, they have learned to use their innate ability to accommodate to new linguistic situations to great effect" (Crystal, 2006: 176).

5.2.1. Classroom norms

It has been noted in the literature that SL breaks down the boundaries of classroom norms and hierarchical behaviour commonly associated with teacher-led lessons. However, the data presents somewhat contrasting results to this notion. Whilst the lesson tasks were designed to embody constructivist approaches, with the belief that a learner-centred lesson will benefit the learners more than of a teacher-led session, the participants' long conditioned schema of classroom behavioural norms are resilient to change even in this virtual environment with those who have never shared the experience of face-to-face learning in a traditional classroom setting (Nesson and Nesson, 2008).

In terms of teacher control, which uncovered one of the more predominant themes in analysis – *power relationships* – the results show that most of topic control by the teacher occurred on occasions when the learners were not contributing actively to the discussions. This in turn, may have had an effect on power relations. Despite this, results retrieved from the later part of the session showed that learners began to mirror earlier turns taken by the teacher – that of positive reinforcement and taking interest in their interlocutor's utterances by asking questions and signalling involvement with less dependency on teacher contributions. Thus, it can be argued that the teacher's involvement – actively facilitating discussion and highlighting prominent points raised by the learners for further engagement – is important for effective socialisation and group development, and encourages autonomy, particularly at the beginning of a course.

The conversation tasks employed in this SL session are simple examples of how SL can be used for geographically dispersed learners in an introductory lesson. There was a conscious effort to avoid overwhelming the participants with more sophisticated task types and help them to acclimatise to the new surroundings. The participants were, therefore, adept in engaging in meaningful negotiation without the hindrance of technological glitches. These have been shown to have a negative impact on a number of SL situated studies (Berge, 2008; de Freitas et al., 2010; Keskitalo et al., 2011; Love et al., 2009; Petrakou, 2010; Sherblom et al., 2009).

The free-flowing, topic-emerging, meaning-focused conversational tasks did not display many significant results of paralinguistic conversational strategy use specific to CMC environments such as 'emoticons' – text symbols used to convey emotions or attitudes. Observations also show that participants did not use the gestures which SL provides. Whilst no strong conclusions or generalisations can be made because only one SL session was chosen for analysis, a possible explanation could be that SL provided the participants with enough in terms of expression and emotional state through the use of voice, text chat and visual affordances. However, according to Deutschman and Panichi, "[t]his type of behaviour is simply so built into our make-up that we do not even reflect over it" (2009: 325).

There was also limited strategy use specific to cognitive development partly because no form-focus activities or tasks were implemented (Long, 1996). Despite the absence of cognitively challenging, problem-solving tasks, the data shows that the activities did encourage an increase in the use of strategies for the negotiation of meaning, organised turn allocation and opportunities for effective conversational management, such as conformation checks and clarification requests. Such tactics according to Pica (1994 cited in Mitchel and Myles 2004: 167) are used specifically to "solve on-going communication difficulties" to "maximise comprehension, and negotiate their way through trouble spots" (ibid.). The data also presented many instances of self-repair and restructuring which, in turn, are strategies concomitant to effective language acquisition.

It is evident from the construction of knowledge between participants and the facilitation and assistance from a native speaker or more competent interlocutor, together with continued support from peers, that such interactions correspond to Thorn's argument on sociocultural theory. It is through sociality that social reality and individual cognitive development are constructed – "language as socially constructed rather than intrinsically intrinsic, language as both referential and constructive of social reality, and notions of distributed and assisted activity in contrast to individual accomplishment" (2000: 227).

5.2.2. Technology and cognitive change

The data has also offered insight into a paradigm shift in cognitive development within the practices of use in communicative activity in SCMC environments. This therefore has an effect on the nature of communicative practice and how interaction is evolving through technological means and multi-modalities. It allows us to re-shape how we think and learn to best meet our specific goals or solve a particular problem, particularly in this virtual environment, where visually, social encounters are altered and conversational subtleties from body language are absent. In addition, according to Carr in his discussion on the progress of technology, "sometimes our tools do what we tell them to. Other times, we adapt ourselves to our tools' requirements" (2011: 47).

It was noted that the immersive qualities of SL offer residents an experience of human-to-human interactions similar to physical reality which relate to the later part of Carr's statement. This was particularly evident from participant feedback; "I feel we sit together to talk. We are in a group (.) eh we are a team, so I feel warm. I feel relaxed to talk with all of you". The feedback by this participant also acknowledged the technical hindrances; however, they were overcome without debilitating difficulties. This shows that the immersive feelings within this virtual platform might outweigh the negatives in order to feel a part of a small community and feel a sense of social presence.

In terms of cognitive change, this session in SL highlighted interesting results in the use of text and voice modalities. Not only do the results from text chat use support ideas of "noticing, consciousness-raising and attention" (Mitchel and Myles, 2004: 173), they also shed light on organised participation and social presence during discussion. Where unconscious use of paralinguistic signals is absent, text chat provided the group members with a means of subtly contributing to conversation, signalling engagement without interfering or inhibiting the flow of the speaker's turn.

5.3. *Teacher reflections*

The use of recordings for analysis of language usage during this SL session proved itself to be an affordance of this virtual environment, which would otherwise have proven difficult in face-to-face situations. The ease of data recording in this environment offers benefits not only for the learners, but also for teacher reflections on teaching practise. According to Meskill et al. "[w]hen incidental learning happens in [face-to-face] classrooms, it can derail the course of the conversation by diverting attention" (2005: 99). This happens particularly when an interlocutor or a learner utters an unfamiliar word and a learner's wishes it to be spelled out; the flow of conversation is broken. However, the functionality of recording SL sessions offers language educators and facilitators the affordance to notice problems that occur through language output and errors made which may have been missed during fast flowing conversations.

SL offers educators the facility to assess student learning in more depth and assess the emerging problems the learners experienced which may have been overlooked or ignored during the live lesson. This way, the teacher has an increased opportunity to "tailor guidance and feedback to individual learners needs and scaffold the use of new forms, vocabulary items and language functions when the opportunity to do so presented itself in online conversations" (Meskill and Anthony, 2005: 102).

Chapter 6: Conclusion

6.1. Limitations and future research

The fundamentally encouraging findings in this small-scale exploratory case study provide evidence that SL appears to be an effective language learning platform for learners to engage in conversation in small groups. However, whilst this study provided an initial inquiry into the nature of communication strategy use in SL and how documenting linguistic development among learners can benefit educators in providing effective language instruction, it is not without its limitations. It must be acknowledged, initially, that there is potentially a high dropout rate when researching in an online environment particularly when the study aims to examine language use by participants who are geographically dispersed. In this present study, time was one of the main reasons participants withdrew from the study. Therefore, future research will consider all facets of sampling before undertaking the research to examine language use within culturally diverse groups. Secondly, because of the modest number of participants who took part in the study, the conclusions will benefit from additional research.

The study only examined one SL session and whilst this represents a limitation, the findings did offer insight into areas that are of interest to be explored in greater depth in future research. In order to achieve more validating conclusions to second language development through learner interactions, a more extended study is required to offer more conclusive results. The implementation of a mixed-methods design for the interpretation of data will allow the measurement of "trends, prevalence's, *(sic)* and outcomes and at the same time examine meaning context and process" (Creswell and Clark, 2007: 175) in the belief that it will "enhance understanding of the phenomenon and allow for a better, more rigorous methodology" (Cresswell and Clark, 2007: 175).

Other limitations, such as technological glitches were also present, although they were overcome quickly within this particular session. However, they may have had a more negative impact if larger groups were used as the objects of the study. Therefore future research should aim to obtain a larger sample, but maintain small group constructions, and implement tasks to examine the effectiveness of learner-centred problem-solving tasks compared with teacher-facilitated communicative instruction. Future study should also attempt to examine how power relations can affect second language learners' participation. Such study should gradually implement more sophisticated and innovative task types, thereby exploiting the myriad of immersive opportunities SL can offer. More focus needs to be placed on the affordances offered in SL, in particular; the way participants adapt their behaviour to the combination of text and voice-enabled functions and how they support and enhance language development during interactions.

Overall, the findings presented by this case study suggest that teacher facilitation and continued support are important to engage learners in the virtual environment, adapt to the new surroundings and encourage them to take risks, thus taking control of their learning. However, further research still needs to be conducted with a focus on interactions between culturally diverse L2 learners, as well as into the potential of SL for language teaching and learning. In that light, hopefully, the presen study will encourage others to undertake the research opportunities presented.

References

Anderson, J. F., Beard, F. K., & Walther, J. B. (2010). Turn-taking and the Local Management of Conversation in a Highly Simultaneous Computer-Mediated Communication System. *Language@Internet*, 7(1), 1 – 28.

Ball, S. & Pearce, R. (2009). Inclusion Benefits and Barriers of "Once-Removed" Participation, in Wankel, C. & Kingsley. J. *Higher Education in Virtual Worlds Teaching and Learning in Second Life*. Bingley: Emerald Group Publishing Limited.

Baralt, M., & Gurzynski-Weiss, L. (2011). Comparing learners' state anxiety during task-based interaction in computer-mediated and face-to-face communication. *Language Teaching Research*, 15(2), 201 – 229.

Bax, S. (2011). *Discourse and Genre: Analysing Language in Context*. Hampshire: Palgrave Macmillan.

Berge, Z. L. (2008). Multi-user virtual environments for education and training? A critical review of Second Life. *Educational Technology*, 48(3), 27 – 31.

Bialystock, E. (1990). *Communication Strategies: A Psychological Analysis of Second Language Use*. London: Blackwell.

Brown, S. (2008). How to connect technology and passion in the service of learning. The Chronicle of Higher Education, October 17. Available from: http://chronicle.com/weekly/v55/i08/08a09901.htm [Accessed 14 June 2011].

Burnett, R. (2009). *Learning to Learn in a Virtual World.* [Online]. Available from: www.learndev.org/dl/burnett_f.pdf [Accessed 31 July 2011].

Campbell, C. (2009). Learning in a different life: Pre-service education students using an online virtual world. *Journal of Virtual Worlds Research,* 2(1), 3 – 17.

Carr, N. (2010). *The Shallows: How the Internet is Changing the way we Read, Think and Remember.* London: Atlantic Books.

Cohen, L., Manion, L., & Morrison, K. (2006). *Research Methods in Education.* (6th ed.) Oxon: Routledge.

Conrad, D. (2002). Engagement, excitement, anxiety, and fear: Learners' experiences of starting an online course. *The American Journal of Distance Education,* 16(2), 205 – 226.

Creswell, J.W., & Clark, V. L. (2007). *Designing and Conducting Mixed Methods Research.* London: SAGE publications Ltd.

Crystal, D. (2006). *Language and the Internet.* Cambridge: Cambridge University Press.

de Freitas, S., Rebolledo-Mendez, G., Liarokapis, F., Magoulas, G., & Poulovassilis, A. (2010). Learning as Immersive Experiences: Using the Four-Dimensional Framework for Designing and Evaluating Immersive Learning Experiences in a Virtual World, *British Journal of Education,* 41(1), 69 – 85.

Deutschmann, M., & Panichi, L. (2009). Talking into empty space? Signalling involvement in a virtual language classroom in Second Life. *Language Awareness,* 18(3), 310 – 328.

Deutschmann, M., Panichi, L., & Molka-Danielsen, J. (2009). Designing oral participation in Second Life – a comparative study of two language proficiency courses. *ReCALL, 21*(02), 206 – 228.

Dreyer, E. & Oxford, R. (1996). Learning strategies and other predictors of ESL proficiency among Afrikaans speakers in South Africa, in Oxford, R. *Language learning strategies around the world: Cross-cultural perspectives.* (Eds.) Honolulu: University of Hawai'i.

Ellis, R. (1994). *Study of Second Language Acquisition.* Oxford: Oxford University Press.

Epp, E. M., Green, K. F., Rahman, A. M., & Weaver, G. C. (2010). Analysis of Student-Instructor Interaction Patterns in Real-Time Scientific Online Discourse. *J Sci Educ Technol, 19*(1), 49 – 57.

Foster, P., & Ohta, A. S. (2005). Negotiation for meaning and peer assistance in second language classrooms. *Applied Linguistics,* 26(3), 402 – 430.

Franceschi, K., Lee, R. M., Zanakis, S. H., & Hinds, D. (2009). Engaging group E-Learning in virtual Worlds. *Journal of Management Systems,* 26(01), 73 – 100.

Girvan, C., & Savage, T. (2010). Identifying an Appropriate Pedagogy for Virtual Worlds: A Communal Constructivism Case Study. *Computers & Education,* 55, 342 – 349.

Gu, N., Gul, L. F., Williams, A., & Nakapan, W. (2009). Second Life – A Context For Design Learning, in Wankel, C. and Kingsley, J. *Higher Education in Virtual Worlds: Tea Teaching and Learning in Second Life.* Bingley: Emerald Group Publishing Limited.

Henderson, M., Huang, H., Grant, S., & Henderson, L. (2009). *Language acquisition in Second Life: Improving self-efficacy beliefs*, 464 – 474.

Hockly, N., & Clandfield, L. (2010). *Teaching Online: Tools and Techniques, Options and Opportunities.* Surrey: DELTA PUBLISHING.

Hundsberger, S. (2009). *Foreign Language Learning in Second Life and implications for resource provision in academic libraries*, [online]. Available from: http://arcadiaproject.lib.cam.ac.uk, [Accessed 16 May 2011].

Hurd, S. (2007). Anxiety and non-anxiety in a distance language learning environment: The distance factor as a modifying influence. *Science Direct*, 35 (1), 487– 508.

Hutchby, I. (2001). *Conversation and Technology: From the Telephone to the Internet.* Oxford: Blackwell.

Jarmon, L., & Sanchez, J. (2008). The educators coop experience in Second Life: A model for collaboration. *Journal of the Research Center for Educational Technology*, 4(2), 66 – 82.

Jarmon, L., Traphagan, T. W., Traphagan, J. W., & Eaton, L. J. (2009). Aging, Lifelong Learning, and the Virtual World of Second Life, in Wankel, C. & Kingsley, J. *Higher Education in Virtual Worlds: Teaching and Learning in Second Life.* Bingley: Emerald Group Publishing Limited.

Jauregi, K., Canto, S., Graaff, R. de, Koenraad, T., & Moonen, M. (2011). Verbal interaction in Second Life: towards a pedagogic framework for task design. *Computer Assisted Language Learning*, 24 (1), 77 – 101.

Keskitalo, T., Pyykko, E. and Ruokamo, H. (2011). Exploring the Meaningful Learning of Students in Second Life. *Educational Technology & Society, 14* (1), 16 – 26.

Kingsley, J., & Wankel, C (2009). *Higher Education in Virtual Worlds: Teaching and Learning in Second Life.* (Eds.). Bingley: Emerald Group Publishing Limited.

Lantolf, J. P. (2000). *Sociocultural Theory and Second Language Learning.* (Eds.) Oxford: Oxford University Press.

Lee, L. (2001). Online interaction: Negotiation of meaning and strategies used among learners of Spanish. *ReCALL, 13*(2), 232 – 44.

Lin, H., & Fang, Y.-C. (2010). EFL learners Perceptions of Computer Mediated Communication (CMC) to Facilitate Communication in a Foreign Language. *World Academy of Science, Engineering and Technology,* 66(1), 714 – 721.

Love, E., Ross, S. C., & Wilhem, W. (2009). Opportunities and Challenges for Business Education in Second Life, in Wankel, C. & Kingsley, J. *Higher Education in Virtual Worlds: Teaching and Learning in Second Life.* Bingley: Emerald Group Publishing Limited.

Meskill, C., & Anthony, N. (2005). Foreign language learning with CMC: forms of online instructional discourse in a hybrid Russian class. *Science Direct, 33*(1) 89 – 105.

Mikropoulos, T. A., & Natsis, A. (2011). Educational virtual environments: A ten-year review of empirical research, *Computers & Education* 56(1) 769 – 780.

Mitchell, R., & Myles, F. (2004). *Second Language Learning Theories* (2nd ed.). London: Hodder Education.

Molka-Danielsen, J., Deutschmann, M., & Panichi, L. (2009). Designing Transient Learning Spaces in Second Life: A case study based on the Kamimo experience. *Design for Learning* 2(1), 22 – 33.

Morse, S., Littleton, F., Macloed, H., & Ewins, R. (2009). The Theatre of Performance Appraisal: Role-Play in Second Life, in Wankel, C. & Kingsley, J. *Higher Education in Virtual Worlds: Teaching and Learning in Second Life.* (Eds.). Bingley: Emerald Group Publishing Limited.

Nesson, R., & Nesson, C. (2008). The case for education in virtual Worlds. *Space and Culture,* 11(3), 273 – 284.

Omale, N., Hung, W-C., Luetkehans, L., & Cooke-Plagwitz, J. (2009). Learning in 3-D multi-user virtual environments: Exploring the use of unique 3-D attributes for online problem-based learning. *British Journal of Educational Technology,* 40(3), 480 – 495.

O'Malley, J. & Chamot, A. (1990). *Learning Strategies in Second Language Acquisition.* Cambridge: Cambridge University Press.

Overbaugh, R. C., & Lin, S. (2006). Student characteristics, sense of community, and cognitive achievement in web-based and lab-based learning environments. *Journal of Research on Technology in Education,* 39(2), 205 – 223.

Oxford, R. (2003). Language Learning Styles and Strategies: An Overview. *Learning Styles & Strategies, GALA* 1 – 25.

Pegrum, M. (2009). *From Blogs to Bombs: The Future of Digital Technologies in Education.* Crawley, Western Australia: UWA Publishing.

Peterson, M. (2009). Learner Interaction in synchronous CMC: a sociocultural perspective. *Computer assisted Language Learning* 22(4), 303 – 321.

Peterson, M. (2010). Learner participation patterns and strategy use in Second Life: an exploratory study. *ReCALL* 22(3), 273 – 292.

Petrakou, A. (2010). Interacting through avatars: Virtual worlds as a context for online education. *Computers & Education* 54(1), 1020 – 1027.

Punch, K.F. (2009). *Introduction to Research Methods in Education.* London: SAGE Publications Ltd.

Ranalli, J. (2008). Learning English with The Sims: exploiting authentic computer simulation games for L2 learning. *Computer Assisted Language Learning,* 21(5), 441 – 455.

Robinson, M., & Carrington, V. (2009). *Digital Literacies: Social Learning and Classroom Practices.* London: SAGE Publications.

Robson, C. (2002). *Real World Research* (2nd ed.). Oxford: Blackwell Publishers Ltd.

Rosenburg, A. (2010). Virtual World Research Ethics and the Private/Public Distinction. *International Journal of Internet Research Ethics,* 3(12), 23 – 36.

Salmon, G. (2009). The future for (second) life and learning. *British Journal of Educational Technology,* 40(3), 526 – 538.

Salmon, G. (2011). *E-moderating: The Key to Teaching and Learning online* (3rd ed.). London: Routledge.

Schiller, S. Z. (2009). Practicing Learner-Centered Teaching: Pedagogical Design and Assessment of a Second Life Project. *Journal of Information Systems Education* 20(3), 369 – 381.

Schmidt, R. (1990). The role of consciousness in second language learning. *Applied Linguistics* 11(1), 129 – 158.

Senior, R. (2010). Connectivity: A Framework for Understanding Effective Language Teaching in Face-to-Face and Online Learning Communities. *RELC Journal* 41(2), 137 – 147.

Shengming, Y. (2009). *The Pragmatic Development of Hedging in EFL Learners.* Ph. D City University of Hong Kong. [online]. Available at: http://dspace.cityu.edu.hk/bitstream/2031/5731/2/fulltext.html [Accessed 15 July 2011].

Sherblom, J. C., Withers, L. A., & Leonard, L. G. (2009). Communication Challenges and opportunities for Educators Using Second Life, in Wankel, C. & Kingsley, J. *Higher Education in Virtual Worlds: Teaching and Learning in Second Life.* (Eds.). Bingley: Emerald Group Publishing Limited.

Silverman, D. (2001). *Interpreting Qualitative Data: Methods for Analysing Talk, Text and Interaction* (2nd ed.). London: SAGE Publications.

Smith, B. (2003). The use of communication strategies in computer-mediated communication. *Science Direct* 31(1), 29 – 53.

Stake, R. E. (1995). *The Art Of Case Study Research.* London: SAGE Publications Ltd.

Tarone, E. (1981). Some Thoughts on the Notion of Communication Strategy. *Tesol Quarterly* 15(3), 285 – 295.

Thorne, S. L. (2000). Second language acquisition theory and the truth(s) about relativity, in Lantolf, J. P. *Sociocultural Theory and Second Language Learning.* Oxford: Oxford University Press.

Van Leir, L. (2000). From input to affordance: Social-interactive learning from an ecological perspective, in Lantolf, J. P. *Sociocultural Theory and Second Language Learning.* Oxford: Oxford University Press.

Vygotsky, L. S. (1978). *Mind in Society: The development of Higher Psychological Processes* Cambridge, MA: Harvard University Press.

Walther, J., Loh, T., & Granka, L. (2005). Let me count the ways: Interchange of verbal and nonverbal cues in computer mediated and face-to-face affinity. *Journal of Language and Social Psychology,* 24(1), 36 – 65.

Wang, X., Song, H., Stone, D.E., & Yan, Q. (2009). Integrating Second Life into Research Collaboration across the Continents. *TechTrends,* 53(6).

Warburton, S. (2009). Second Life in higher education: Assessing the potential for and the barriers to deploying virtual worlds in learning and teaching. *British Journal of Educational Technology,* 40(3), 414 – 427.

Warschauer, M. (1996). Comparing Face-to-Face and Electronic Communication in the Second Language Classroom. *CALICO Journal,* 13(1), 17 – 26.

Warschauer, M. (2002). On-line Communication in Carter, R. & Nunan, D. *The Cambridge Guide to Teaching English to Speakers of Other Languages* Cambridge: Cambridge University Press.

Warschauer, M. (2007). The paradoxical future of digital learning. *Learning Inquiry*, 1(1), 41 – 49.

Wenger, E. (1998). *Communities of practice*. Cambridge: Cambridge University Press.

Wenger, E., White, N., & Smith, J. D. (2009). *Digital Habitats: Stewarding technology for communities.* Portland: CPsquare.

Williams, E. (1998). *Research and Paradigms*, [online]. MComms programme at Victoria University of Wellington. Available at http://www.umdnj.edu/idsweb/idst6000/williams_research+paradigms.htm, [Accessed 17 July 2011].

Wong, J., & Waring, H. Z. (2010). *Conversation Analysis and Second Language Pedagogy*. Oxon: Routledge.

Yang, Y. -F. (2011). Engaging students in an online situated language learning environment. *Computer Assisted Language Learning*, 24(2), 181 – 198.

Yin, R. K. (2003). *Case study research: design and methods* (2nd ed.). Thousand Oaks, CA: Sage Publications.

Yule, E., & Tarone, E. (1997). Investigating communication strategies in L2 reference: Pros and cons, in Kasper, G. & Kellerman, E. (Eds.), *Communication strategies: Psycholinguistics and sociolinguistic perspectives.* London: Longman.

Appendices

A1: Short course application form

The teacher who conducted the lessons in the short course, and who was also a participant in the study, designed and issued this questionnaire to all potential participants. It was used to identify suitable applicants who could offer the time, computer capacity and linguistic abilities required for the success of the course.

Thank you for taking an interest in this course. Please answer the questions below so I can decide whether this course can benefit you.
What's your name? (Please also write your Email address)
How old are you?
What is your level of English?
Are you available from the 1st to the 30th of June?
Do you have any holidays planned in June? Please let me know what dates you are not available.
How many hours per week can you dedicate to this course?
Are you available on weekends?
To participate in this course it will require you to download some software therefore a high computer bandwidth and a fast Internet connection are imperative. Do you fit these needs?
Do you use of Second Life (a virtual world)? **If yes – What do you use it for? (Please answer fully)** **If no – Have you heard of it before? (Please answer fully)**
What are your expectations from this course? Please answer fully.

How much time do you spend on each of the following in a typical week?

	0 to 3 hours	4 to 5 hours	6 to 9 hours	10 to 14 hours	More than 15 hours
Email					
Instant Messenger					
Social Networking sites (Facebook, My Space, QQ etc.)					
Word processing (Microsoft Word)					
Other					

If you checked 'Other' in the question above, please state here:

I am very comfortable using a computer to communicate with others. *

	1	2	3	4	5	
Strongly agree						Strongly disagree

I enjoy using a computer to communicate with others *

1 = I enjoy it very much 5= I don't enjoy it at all

	1	2	3	4	5	
Strongly agree						Strongly disagree

Background information

Thank you taking the time to complete this form. Now all that is required is for you to provide the following information (your answers will remain anonymous and won't be shown to anyone unrelated to this research project).

Your Name: *

Your Occupation: *

Your Native Language: *

Where do you live? City/Town: *

State/Province:

Country: *

Email Address:

A2: Transcript of Second Life Session One (abridged)

S = Student; T = Teacher

S1: hahaha ye, I do go to the karaoke sometimes so... Hahaha that's quite cool, I like that/

T: Do they have Karaoke in Germany?

S1: not in a lot of places, only um the Irish bar in my my em in my town does it. So they have every Thursday and every Saturday in the summer so that it's convenient. /

T: Right/ em S2, do you like to go to Karaoke? /

S2: Yes, yes, we often go to karaoke and sing mm the songs sing uhhh the songs I like. Umm but, do often go to karaoke? Some of my foreign friends told me uh uh tell me that they don't go to karaoke often they don't like uhhh singing front of uh lots of people. They they prefer more to they prefer to go to a bar uh to drink, of dance uhh with people. / How about you? /

T: ah I see/

S1: I think most of the people I know they don't they do like to go to karaoke, but they don't like to sing themselves ... hehehe... cos they are so embarrassed. //

S2: Oh, I see//

S1: ye, but I it's a lot of fun, I mean if people go and stage they can't really sing, but then they are good laugh so um you enjoy yourselves as well. //

T: great and, do you sing German songs or English songs or both?

S2: emm mostly it's English songs they have a few / German songs on karaoke where I go to, but they're not really my ki..cup of tea..he hehe

T: Ha haha

S1: They are most… have you heard about Shlagar music?

T: Can you repeat that?

S1: heard about Schlaaaga music, like em

T: Schlaga?

S1: so it's like, em… I don't know..sort of ..[laughing]I can't find an expression..to [laughing whilst speaking not understandable]

T: hahaha..how do you spell it?

S1: em..[Typing in local chat]/ Schlager

T: schlager

S1: so it's like em// le people like to listen to or to dance to, so if you're havin a party it can be really nice but most of the times I don't like it heheheh

T: ahhhh I see

S2: of course, you just said it's for old people.

T: haha

S2: yeye and beautiful of course you won't like it hahahaha

S1: I, I know people my age who love Schlager so um it's not really an age thing but a matter of taste I think hehehehe //

S2: okay okay sorry I don't know about that

S1: wow that's a lot to think

T: Ah I see… S1 do you have any questions about eh S3's headline? /

S1: Well it sounds very multi tasking to me hehehe

[All are laughing]

S1: You're going eh eh to em ye if you having so much direction you'd like to go what what what interests you in founding a company then?

S3: A company? /

S1: Didn't you say eh you're thinking about found a company on your own? Em to be self-employed or anything?

S3: ye ah I'm thinking about to eh set up a company a foreign trade company eh to do my own business eh but there is some difficulties eh in front so (shh) I haven't decided

S1: Oh I see, here is the same as well first you have to raise the money and then you have to have em the connections as well, haven't you?

S3: ye so mmm this time money is the big problem for me (small laugh and sigh) and em

S1: (INAUDABLE) //

S3: hello

S1: so em what would your business be then? //

S3: Foreign trade

T: Ah foreign trade? /

S1: ok.

S3: foreign trade

S1: wow

T: what type of things would you trade? //

S3: I think eh about eh shoes? Or in electronic product eh and eh

S1: (can't make out what she said) something like, "go for the shoes! hahah"

(All laughed)

T: hahaha

S3: China China is the manufacture factory of the world you know? Eh most shoes in the world was produced in China

S2: Yes Yes many in (CITY IN CHINA 1) right?

S1: yeah?

S3: yeah (CITY IN CHINA 1) and eh (CITY IN CHINA 2)

T: I take it you like shoes S1?

S2: yeah /

S1: Ye I do like shoes hehehe

(all laugh)

S3: So if eh if you have any need of these eh I think we will have a opportunity to cooperate

T: Everything is made in China

S1: Oh yes I'll be your first customer heheheheh

[all laugh]

S3: perfect hehehe

T: is it only only female shoes that you would trade or do you think you would trade with men's shoes also?

S3: Both both sure both

T: AH Cool do you do you have any questions?, S2…

S1: but the women's anyway, coz' they buy more shoes don't they?

S2: yes so I can see from your headline eh it's about eh your career plans, so my question is what's your top priority when you make eh decision about your career. Eh it's em you will eh take a like eh your career development, your interests or just money into consideration? What's your top priority?

S3: eh mostly the most important is eh eh my interest /

T: brilliant question /

S1: sorry

T: what is your main interest, S3?

S2: yeah what is your interest

S3: My interest is eh contact with people and eh learning eh from (shh) ah learning from a other peoples eh other foreign peoples

T: I see

S3: My interest

S1: just like me lol

S2: yes I got it! Me too I love it!

S3: hehe Thank you!

S2: you know I...

T: We all have similar interests

S2: yes

S1: Seems like ye

T: Perfect! /

T: nice one! ... so S3

S2: S3? S3? Now eh have you heard it out eh what will you going to do in the future? What's your another way? Hehe

S3: Another way eh another way is to find another company another foreign trade company in (PLACE NAME) eh and eh gain more experience on this and finally I think I will go on the way to start my own company. Start my own business

T: great

T: Stress can sometimes be good

S1: o that's awful

S3: ... not good for me then I ah make it clear life life is life work is work eh do not bring work...

S2: otherwise I will be as lazy as possible

S3: ... to ah to my (shh) eh spare time so when I work I...

S1: yeah I agree

S3: ... try my best to do that to make everything right but eh when I off work I ehh not eh try to eh forget what I done what I have done ah in the day night (shh) eh so it well easy my ten..tennis I will sleep eh well much well in the night

S1: oh yeah I see I have that as well I was lying in bed an eh thinking about a problem I had at work hehe that's not really good is it?

T: good technique S3 //

T: yeah it's helpful advice you have

S1: ye, I think that's good coz' em...

S3: thank

S1: ... leaving work to work...

T: Helpful advice

S1: ... and then you have your spare time is it?

S2: hello I have reading interesting news about stress. Do you know what is the most stressful time? Ehhhh in the week?

T: Work can be too time consuming

S2: ... It's 8am in Monday you know

T: yeah... I can imagine

S2: it it says that ye a...

S1: hahah

S2: Study of 11,000..

T: hahahaha

S2: [unrecognizable word] proved 8am on Monday morning is the most stressful time or the heart and the and ...

S2: I agree

S2: ..[... day?] is the least stressful day with the fewest heart attacks? You know do we know why Monday morning is so stressful coz' working people get up on Monday there blood pressure and heart rate go up aaaand all these things can have an unfavorable effect on the...

S1: what is the less stress day again?

S2: ... in the bood system and increase the risk of a clot which will cause a heart attack so be careful on Monday morning

[all laugh]

S3: Yeah! On Monday I have experience on Monday (shh) eh ehhhevery things comes to you hehe everythings come to you and you are busy in dealing and em make eh make sure (shh) eh everything will go right ah so eh we feel pressure that we feel very tired on Monday, but Friday is a good day

[All laugh]

S1: Friday is less stress day is it?

S2: yes

S1: I didn't get that

T: Monday blues

S1: hahaha

T: Friday feeling

S2: And when it but when it's Monday mmm you will have you will have a hard workload more stress more anger and more physical activities [deep breath] it's so awful, painful. I really hate Monday

T: yeah... what about Sunday evening? Thinking about Monday morning

S1: worse heheheh

[All laugh]

S2: oh it's worse

S1: I try not to I try not to but I don't succeed every time

S3: yeah hehe /

T: It's difficult to do

S2: I cannot sleep well each Sunday light each sun eh each Sunday lights eh light

S3: Why?

S3: Why?

S2: Too stressful

S3: stressful? For study or? Anything else?

S2: about about the morning feelings

T: Sunday night is a problem. anticipation of the Monday blues

S3: but eh the senior student...

S1: I know that too. specially if im on an early shift

S2: yes

T: yeah so even if you even if you are studying on the Monday is it still stressful S2?

S2: yes

S3: agree /

T: ok that was great. It was really nice hearing your own headlines your personal headline it's really interesting so thanks for sharing that with us

S1: like

A3: Focus group: short question and answer session

S = Student; T = Teacher; R = Researcher

R: What are your opinions about studying or practicing your English in SL from your experience so far?

S3: Ye, I think it is a perfect idea and eh we got some difficulties eh such as internet connection eh time arranged problem

S2: I can enjoy a lot of freedom ye I can I can em and a lot of freedom of making mistakes and free from you know serious judgment or remarks from the teachers. You know studying English in SL actually we don't have eh English teachers, so you can you can try to ehm show eh try to practice your English coz em without the help of your English teacher or classmates so I think SL ehm is better for you to eh apply your English knowledge eh the ehmm the English words, phrases you have learnt into your daily conversation, your daily practice and eh that's it.

S1: you got us talking alright! (Text chat)

S1: It's not a classroom; it's more like a conversation. It's not like studies really, so I really enjoy it

R: What were your expectations of SL before your first visit? What did you expect to get from SL before you came here?

S2: before I came to SL I have no idea what second life is. I've never heard about it before, so I think I have no expectations, but the moment I come to SL mmmmm
I just, I just, I just make eh a UN plan for myself coz a lot of people come from different places, different countries all play SL so my UN plan is to see and talk with, you know, peoples from different countries and know about their culture and countries and hopefully I get some chances to eh visit their eh countries. That's my UN plan. // Also, I can, I can practice my English.

S1: *Me neither, I haven't heard about SL before*

R: What sort of things would you like to do in future sessions? If you can think of anything that you can possibly do, what kind of things might interest you?

S2: You mean the things I haven't done in SL before?

R: Like, as a group, with your teacher.

S2: Oh as a group? Ehhm I've heard that peoples can do business in SL and make money eh so em if I have time, if
I have a chance, I'd like to eh maybe open a clothes shop mmm in the shopping center with my friends, hehehe and make money and have fun at the same time. Coz eh I heard that some people do that.

S3: good Idea!

S1: I had problems with SL you know, em exploring and how to get in contact with people, so I'd like to do that as a group maybe. If you are more confident in that I'd like maybe it's possible to show how you can use it.

R: Excellent, excellent, I think that's doable. Ok and last Q and please use the text chat for this. Can you think of five adjectives to best describe your thoughts, experiences practicing English in SL?

T: Scary, Fun, challenging, magical

S1: challenging, exciting

S2: cool, thrilling, gorgeous, interesting, informative

S3: free, relax, fun, friendly, and interesting

R: Now that you know SL and you also know Skype, which, in your opinion, is better for group discussion, what do you think?

S1: (text) SL

S2: yes SL

S1: (text) definitely

S3: yes

S2: face to face talk even though its em our (something) face-to-face can provoke your thoughts. We can feel eh, we can mmmm you know let our thoughts flow and talk as much as possible mmmm so SL is better

S3: mmm in my opinion eh Skype and SL both have their advantages eh when taught in Skype we eh I think I will hear your more clear and accurate ummm but in SL sometimes eh the voice is not good enough maybe it is because my computer or my internet connection eh SL have the advantages of eh I agree with S2, face to face talk and I feel we sit together to talk we are in a group eh we are a team so I feel warm, I feel relaxed to talk with all of you and this is my opinion.

A4: Sample of course blog comments

S1 says:

June 22, 2011 at 5:43 pm

Wow [teacher], you expressed my thoughts about SL quite precisely, tho I'm still on the Mission to get started yet. I haven't been to many places in SL, but you really make me curious by this blog. Sometimes I think the virtual world takes so much of our precious time, keeps me inactive on my sofa and I should make a move, go out to meet real people (in a real pub;) – but then again: talk there can be as rubbish, can't it? LOL.

At the moment I can say I loved the safe environment, where we all talked. It was easy to interact, because you know who you dealt with and your support to interact helped a lot. So I think communicating this way helps to become more confident with a language you know quite well, but is different to reading and writing it only.

Thanks for sharing the possibilities of SL here. I'm getting more excited now to explore and find out about music, places (and pubs). Speak later, when I'll be back from my trip.

Teaching EFL Online
An e-moderator's report

by Andrew R. Webster

The Second Life sessions referred to in this book were also the subject of a research paper by Andrew R. Webster. The edited version of this paper is available from LinguaBooks under the title *Teaching EFL Online: An e-moderator's report*.

This book explores the role played by the e-moderator in creating and teaching an online course in English as a Foreign Language. It details relevant theories of online learning and shows how they are represented through various models, creating a framework to assist the e-moderation process. The study includes an analysis of Salmon's five-stage model and critically assesses its effectiveness in helping to prepare a new e-moderator to teach in an online environment.

During the project, qualitative self-study research was carried out and captured by the moderator in the form of an introspective, reflective journal. As the reader will quickly come to appreciate, the author's findings reveal not only the complexities, problems, responsibilities and challenges encountered but also the tremendous rewards that can be gained from the e-moderation process.

www.ingramcontent.com/pod-product-compliance
Lightning Source LLC
Chambersburg PA
CBHW071839090426
42737CB00012B/2302

9781911369509